THE Panel Quilting WORKSHOP

12 QUICK-AND-EASY QUILTING IDEAS FOR EVERY SEASON

Stephanie Soebbing

Landauer Publishing

The Panel Quilting Workshop

Landauer Publishing, *www.landauerpub.com*, is an imprint of Fox Chapel Publishing Company, Inc.

Project Team
Acquisitions Editor: Amelia Johanson
Editor: Madeline DeLuca
Designer: Wendy Reynolds
Photographer: Stephanie Soebbing
Proofreader and Indexer: Kelly Umenhofer

Shutterstock used: Unwanus (page 21).

ISBN 978-1-63981-104-5

Library of Congress Control Number: 2025940429

To learn more about the other great books from Fox Chapel Publishing, or to find a retailer near you, call toll-free 800-457-9112 or visit us at *www.FoxChapelPublishing.com*.

We are always looking for talented authors.

To submit an idea, please send a brief inquiry to acquisitions@foxchapelpublishing.com.

Or write to:
903 Square Street
Mount Joy, PA 17552

Printed in China
First printing

FSC MIX Paper | Supporting responsible forestry FSC® C016973

Introduction

This book exists because of a YouTube tutorial. In July of 2023, I posted a video, "3 Ways to Use a Quilt Panel," on my channel Quilt Addicts Anonymous. I threw it in the editorial calendar as our fun listicle for the month. What I didn't expect was the response, both in views and comments from all of you who had a vast collection of panels and no idea what to do with them. Thus, *The Panel Quilting Workshop* was born.

I took my assignment from you all seriously. I worked to create 12 different designs using quilt panels that range from easy to intermediate quilt designs, easy to designer-quality bag projects, and a number of home décor items that will allow you to create Instagram-worthy, #memade photoshoots.

In this book, I work with all the common sizes and design panels you can currently find in quilt shops from the traditional 24" (61cm) x WOF panel, to 10" (25.4cm) square motifs, and newly possible digitally printed 36" (91.4cm) x WOF designs and placemat panels. You're sure to find ideas on how to make a dent in your panel stash.

I also give you permission to cut up your panels and use them in unexpected ways, or to—gasp!—only use your favorite parts of the panel and make each project your own.

Almost every pattern in this book comes with a video tutorial to help walk you through the steps, so you know the best way to square your panels, fudge it when there's no way they can be square, and a blooper reel that includes me killing a spider in self-defense with a cutting mat. Just scan the QR code with each pattern to watch the free tutorial on *academy.quiltaddictsanonymous.com.*

Happy Quilting,
—Stephanie Soebbing

P.S. Here's the blooper reel!

Contents

32

58

82

38

44

54

62

68

72

90

98

104

All About Quilt Panels

Traditionally, quilt panels were always printed in 24" (61cm) x WOF (width of fabric) cuts, or two-thirds of a yard. This industry standard was set by the rotary screen-printing technology that is used in traditional fabric printing. The designs can only accommodate 24" (61cm) wide repeats, hence the 24" (61cm) panel.

The designs could be anything from the design motifs on a large scale from the fabric yardage to photorealistic landscape scenes. Sometimes you'd find 10" (25.4cm) vignettes that could be fussy cut for block centers, fabric books, soft toy patterns, and even aprons you just have to cut and hem. But, as digital printing technology is becoming more popular in the quilting industry, quilters are seeing more options in panel designs.

Most notably, freed from the 24" (61cm) maximum repeat, designers often opt for 36" (91.4cm), (1-yard) repeats. Practically, it gives us a better proportion for a quilt center and provides six coordinating placemats in one panel instead of four with 24" (61cm) wide panels.

In this book, we work with several different types of panels to give you ideas on how to use your favorites.

There are so many options available when panel quilting.

How to Shop When Buying Quilt Panels

When in doubt and you want to make a quilt, buy:

- ❍ The panel
- ❍ Coordinating fat-quarter bundle
- ❍ ½ yard (45.72cm) for the panel border
- ❍ 3 yards (2.743m) background
- ❍ ¾ yard binding (68.58cm)
- ❍ 4-yard backing (3.65m)

You seriously cannot go wrong with the shopping list above if you come across a panel that you want to turn into a quilt. You will be able to create a large lap quilt with the materials above.

When in doubt and you want to make a bag, buy:

- ❍ The panel
- ❍ ⅔ yard (60.96cm) for lining, 1½ (137.16cm) if you want pockets
- ❍ ½ yard (45.72cm) for handles
- ❍ ⅔ yard (60.96cm) of something else for if you change your mind about anything

When in doubt and you want to make placemats, buy:

- ❍ The panel
- ❍ 1 yard (91.4cm) backing
- ❍ 1 yard (91.4cm) binding (not needed for No-Piecing-Required Placemat)

Now, occasionally you're going to follow my advice above and come up short. Maybe you want your pattern to be larger than a lap. Maybe you want to make the Pieced Placemat and not the No-Piecing-Required Placemat, and mixed up the yardages. But, if you've done at least some of the above, you'll be able to pull it off. Here's a few examples of how I made it work for this book:

I had so much fabric for the 18" (45.72cm) Quilted Panel Throw Pillows (see project on page 32). I knew there was no way I'd be able to feature all of it, plus a panel on the front of the pillow. So, I took as much as I could from the rest and made a design on the back. I still have LOTS of fabric left over, but I got a little bit of everything into the project.

The Alternating Stars Owl pattern (page 104) was one I made using a panel I fell in love with years ago. I somehow ended up with two panels, 8" (20.3cm) of one pink fabric, half a yard (45.7cm) of a multicolor piece, and well over a yard (91.4cm) of a lime-and-yellow print I really didn't love. I made the star points work with what I had of the line, used an ample amount of solid black for the background, and ended up with one of my favorite quilts in the book!

The Vertical Panel Quilt (page 72) has a plain black border and binding. I only had the panel and a fat quarter bundle to make the entire quilt, so I needed every scrap for the blocks. Black and space went together, and I already had it in my stash, so it was a win.

Shop by Fabric Line

The absolute easiest way to make sure every fabric in your quilt perfectly complements your quilt panel is to only use coordinating fabric that was in that fabric line. When panel collections are designed, the panel is often designed first and then elements from the panel are pulled to create the coordinating yardage, often in a less busy setting and on a much smaller scale.

You still have to pay attention to the color value to make the quilt pattern work, but a significant amount of the work is done for you by making sure all the colors and motifs are expertly matched. When I am working by the fabric line, that's when I'm most likely to stick to the lists when I make my initial shopping.

Make it easy on yourself by using coordinating fabric from the same fabric line.

Make It Scrappy

This is the best option to use if you are working with a panel from your stash. We all have them. We thought it was gorgeous, but we didn't get anything to go with it, and now we have one pretty picture and no plan. Here's your new plan:

Step 1. Locate the selvage edge of the panel that has the dots of color in it. Those dots are a listing of all the colors used in the panel.

Step 2. Find as many close matches as possible in your blender and solids categories. Blenders are the fabrics you often find in a "color wall" at a quilt shop. They have very subtle patterns usually in 2–3 colors and can give the fabric design a texture, without detracting from the main focus, which in this case is the panel.

Step 3. Create a cohesive color story from your blenders and solids to support the panel, enhancing its design while keeping the eye on the panel for the final design. You'll want to look critically at how all your fabrics work together and only keep the ones that support without distraction. You may also find that you have a few holes in your color story—that's what you'll want to purchase.

Step 4. Purchase a single background fabric. Trust me, the eye needs a place to rest. Give it one. I've started buying fabric I would use as a quilt background in 4-yard (3.7-m) increments to keep in my stash for these exact moments.

Consider Fabric Yardages as "The Minimum"

The last bit of advice is to treat any fabric requirement as "the minimum" amount needed to complete the project as shown. I'm not talking about rounding up an extra quarter yard if you know you tend to cut wrong. I'm talking about going ahead and splurging on the fat quarter bundle that has 24 fabrics when the pattern only calls for 12 fat quarters, so you can have a greater variety of fabrics in your quilt.

These patterns are just the starting point. Now it's time to put your own spin on the quilt and use as many fabrics as you want.

The selvage edge of a panel has dots of color that list all the colors used in that panel. You can use these dots to create a color story for your project.

Quilting Basics

Watch our
free Beginner
Quilting course!

If you need additional help with basics, or a refresher, you can watch our free Beginner Quilting course on Quilt Addicts Anonymous Academy. The course includes 12 videos and a free pattern walking you through everything you need to know to make your first quilt, from the supplies you need and how to read a pattern, all the way through labeling and caring for your finished quilt.

Essential Tools

If you are just starting out, there are must-have tools, and then there are the additional tools that will make your projects come together faster and easier. Here are some of the essentials you want to consider before getting started, as well as what they do and why you might want to try them.

Sewing Machine

This may seem like a no-brainer, but a machine is the first and most important tool you will need to learn how to quilt. You don't need anything fancy to start. As long as it will sew a straight stitch and is clean, you'll be fine. If you do purchase a new machine, I recommend buying one from a local store where you can learn how to use it and they will service it for you.

Sewing machine.

Binding clips.

Quarter-Inch Presser Foot

Every quilt pattern I've ever read is written for a ¼" (6.4mm) seam allowance. The easiest way to maintain a consistent seam is to use a ¼" (6.4mm) presser foot. Some feet maintain this measurement when the needle is centered, and the seam is sewn along the outer edge of the foot. Other types have a small metal guide to move your fabric along when you are sewing a seam. Machines might come with a dedicated ¼" (6.4mm) foot, or you can purchase one of the available after-market feet.

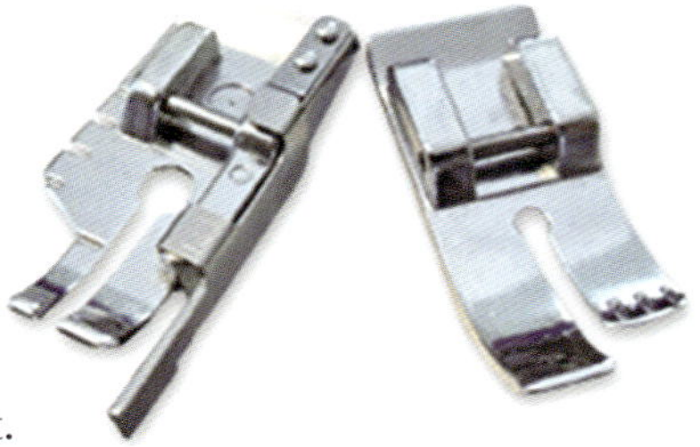

Quarter-inch presser foot.

Walking Foot

Use a walking foot any time you are moving three or more layers through your sewing machine. The walking foot is special because it has small ridges, or "feed dogs," on top of the foot that move in tandem with the feed dogs under the throat plate of your machine. Layers are moved through the machine at the same rate, preventing bunching or puckering.

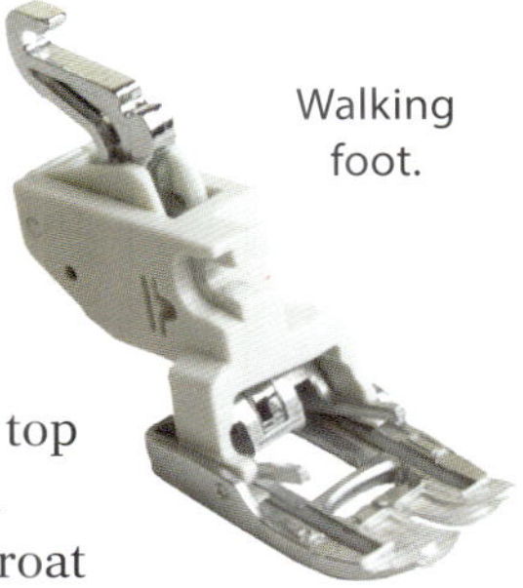

Walking foot.

Binding Clips

When working with seams, backing, and fabric, using binding clips will hold everything in place with no bunching!

Thread

Choosing a good thread can prevent headaches as you sew. Quality thread can help avoid lint build-up, extending the time you can go between cleanings. Also, when you move from piecing to quilting, thread choice plays a powerful role in the finished look of the quilt. For piecing and quilting, I use Aurifil™ 50wt thread. I like to piece with white thread no matter what color of fabric I'm working with, and I use all colors of thread for quilting.

Thread.

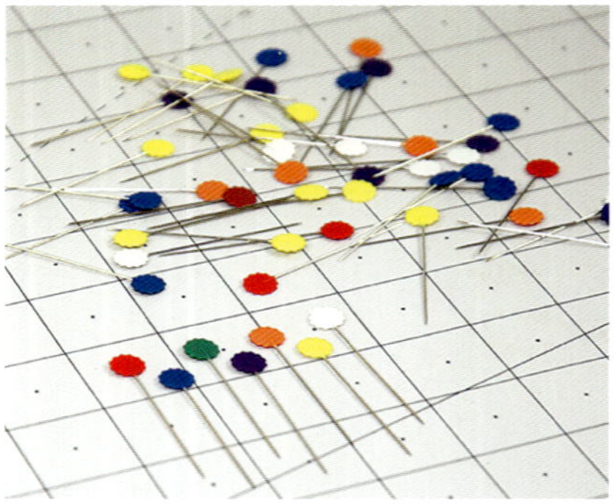

Flower-head pins.

Quilting rulers.

Rotary cutters.

Rotary Cutters

A rotary cutter looks and works like a pizza cutter. A rotary cutter allows you to cut fabric quickly, easily, and accurately with the aid of an acrylic ruler or template. There are many options on the market, but they all do the same thing. A rotary cutter's blade is very sharp, and it can cut quickly and unexpectedly if you aren't careful with it. Always make sure your blade is in the safety setting when you aren't using your rotary cutter.

Cutting Mats

I suggest you buy no smaller than an 18" x 24" (45.72 x 60.96cm) self-healing cutting mat. With that size or larger, you'll be able to cut strips across the width of fabric (WOF), which is required for nearly every pattern in this book. Mats are gridded to assist you in cutting, but it's important to make sure the 1" (2.54cm) squares of the grid are accurate.

Quilting Rulers

Acrylic quilting rulers come in all shapes and sizes, but the 6" x 24" (15.24 x 60.96cm) ruler is one of the most versatile. This ruler spans the width of the folded fabric and can be used to cut strips, squares, and even triangles. Try to find a ruler with 30-, 45-, and 60-degree lines on it, so you can also use it to trim triangle blocks. For smaller cuts, try a 6½" (16.51cm) square or a 2" x 12" (5.08 x 30.48cm) to 4" x 12" (10.16 x 30.48cm) rectangular ruler for cutting, trimming, and squaring up pieces.

Pins

You need something to hold your fabric together as you sew, and pins are that something! I prefer flower-head pins because they slide easily into quilting fabric, they're easy to grab, and they're cute! Try to find long, thin pins for easier handling.

Quilting Fabric

When you start quilting, buy the best fabric you can afford. It will be well worth it in the end. Quilt-shop quality cotton is always worth the money because the thread count is higher, the fabric holds its shape, and it's usually softer.

To choose your fabric, start by finding a focal print that you love, then pick supporting prints that complement the focal fabric. One great way to find coordinating colors is to choose prints from one fabric line. Most lines have 12–24 coordinating prints, so you can't go wrong.

When I'm planning a scrappy quilt, I often choose two colors and raid my stash for fabrics that work in that theme. (Of course, if you're just starting to quilt, you may not have this option.) I recommend buying a neutral to tie them all together. Neutral doesn't mean white or tan. I once made a quilt that used lime green as a neutral!

There is a great debate on whether to prewash your fabric. I never prewash my fabric because the combination of shrinkage and frayed edges often make the piece too small to get all the pieces you need out of it. As long as you purchase quilt-shop quality cotton, your fabric will shrink evenly when you wash your completed quilt the first time, and you won't have to worry about the colors bleeding—although it is a good idea to throw a color-catcher laundry sheet (or three) in the wash with the quilt the first time you wash it, just in case.

Quilting fabric.

Batting.

Batting

Batting is the layer that goes in between the quilt top and backing fabric. It provides warmth and creates texture to the top when quilted. I prefer Quilters Dream® batting and alternate between 100-percent cotton and 80/20 cotton/poly blend. Natural fibers help the cotton quilting fabric stick to the batting, making it easier to keep the fabric from bunching, especially if you are quilting on your home machine.

Another consideration for batting is color. It comes in natural, white, and black. I use white batting if there are white or gray neutrals in my quilt. I like the look of bleached white batting behind these colors. When I am working with a very dark or black background, I opt for black polyester batting. Occasionally bits of batting will get pushed through the quilting stitches, and if you use black batting, you will never see it.

Techniques

This review of basic techniques will make your experience sewing and quilting with panels so much more rewarding.

Perfect Piecing

There are two skills you need to master to create perfect piecing. Accurate cutting is the first, followed by sewing an accurate ¼" (6.4mm) seam. Quilting fabric comes from the store folded in half with the selvages touching. The selvage is the edge on each side of the fabric that prevents it from unraveling. Leave your fabric folded when you start. You will need to straighten the edge that was cut from the bolt. Starting with a straight fabric edge will guarantee accurate cuts.

Straightening the Fabric and Cutting Strips

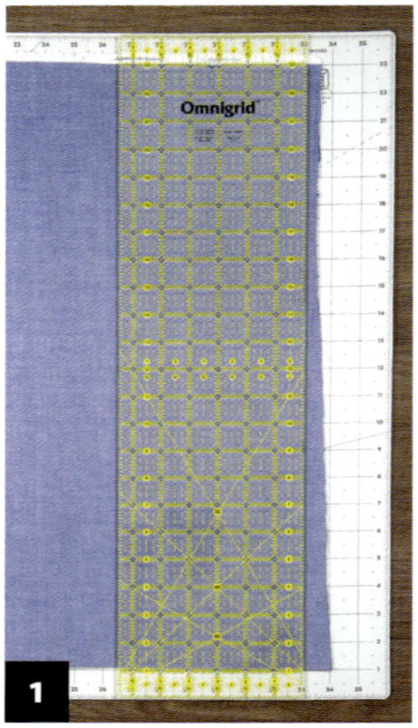

1. Lay the fabric on a cutting mat with the cut side toward the right side of the mat. Smooth out any wrinkles. With the fold at the bottom of the mat, place a 6" x 24" (15.24 x 60.96cm) ruler on the fabric so that it spans the entire width of fabric (WOF). Align the ruler so the 1" (2.54cm) line is even with the fold of the fabric. Extend the fabric beyond the ruler's edge, just enough to straighten the fabric.

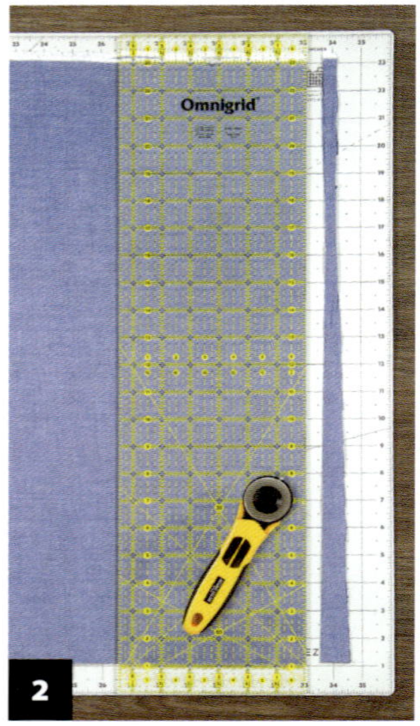

2. Hold the ruler down firmly with the palm of your hand, and use a rotary cutter to cut along the ruler's edge.

3. Flip the fabric to the left side of the cutting mat and realign the ruler on the 1" (2.54cm) line. For example, we're cutting a 3" (7.62cm) strip. Align the 3" (7.62cm) line of the ruler along the straightened edge of the fabric. Repeat Step 2 and cut the strip.

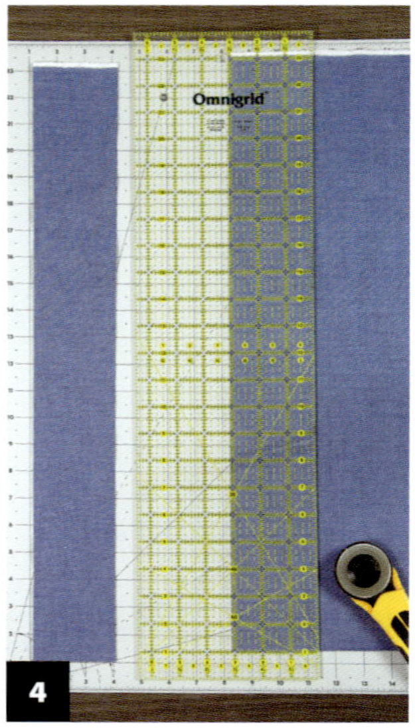

4. Continue cutting strips in this manner. As long as the 1" (2.54cm) line of the ruler is on the fabric fold, and the line of the required strip width aligns along the edge of the fabric, you will have straight, accurate strips. If you are cutting a lot of strips, it's a good idea to occasionally check the fabric edge to make sure it's still straight. Check by repeating Step 1.

Sewing a Seam

The other skill needed for perfect piecing is sewing an accurate ¼" (6.4mm) seam. Not all ¼" (6.4mm) feet are identical, because manufacturers make them specifically for their own sewing machines. If your machine comes with one, that's great. If not, you'll still be able to sew a perfect seam without one.

1. With the needle aligned on the ¼" (6.4mm) line of a ruler, check to see where the edge of your presser foot falls. You can see that this foot won't sew a ¼" (6.4mm) seam.

2. Take a piece of tape and lay it against the edge of the ruler, pressing the tape down on the throat of your machine. Use the edge of the tape as your ¼" (6.4mm) guide.

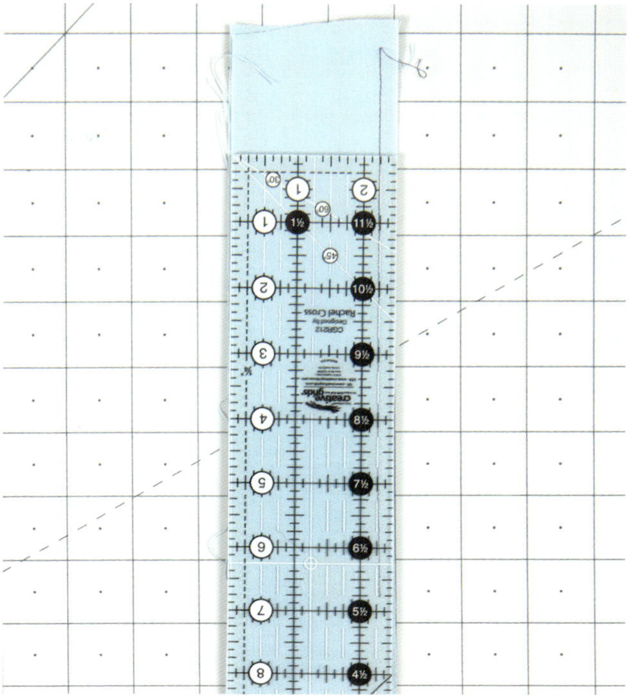

3. However you choose to sew your seam, it's a good idea to check it for accuracy. An extra ⅛" (0.32cm) may not seem like a lot, but those eighths can add up quickly, and you may end up with pieces that do not fit together.

PRO TIP

Some patterns tell you to sew a scant ¼" (6.4mm) seam, for instance, when making half-square triangles. When a half-square triangle is folded open at the seam, it takes up a couple threads. By sewing a couple threads short of the ¼" (6.4mm), you will maintain the correct size of your half-square triangle (HST). See page 16 for how to make HSTs.

Half-Square Triangles

There are many ways to sew half-square triangles, but my favorite way is to make them from squares. I can get two-for-one triangles, and it's easier than sewing individual triangles on the bias because it avoids fabric stretch.

1. Draw a diagonal line from corner to corner on the wrong side of a square. Layer the right sides together with a second square.

2. Sew a scant ¼" (6.4mm) seam on either side of the drawn line.

3. Cut on the drawn line, open, and press the seams.

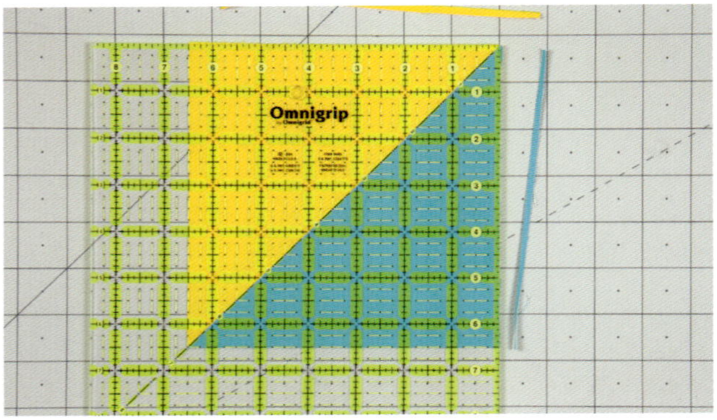

4. Square up the half-square triangles to the measurement in the project.

Fussy Cutting

Fussy cutting is a term that refers to cutting your fabric so that the motif is centered in the middle of the block you are cutting. Typically, this would be used when you have "too-pretty-to-cut-up fabric," where you want to make sure your animal head is centered in your block and not a butt, or a bird with a cut-off wing.

There are many ways to utilize fussy cutting to bring your quilts to the next level, but in this book, we'll use it when we want to cut the panel into parts instead of using it as an entire piece of fabric. You'll find examples of this in Unicorn Love (page 96), the 18" (45.7cm) throw pillows, Alternating Stars (page 104), and even the wrong side of the No-Piecing Placemat (page 68), where I made one of the duplicate placemats double-sided.

Here's how to make sure you can center your design each time to get fantastic results.

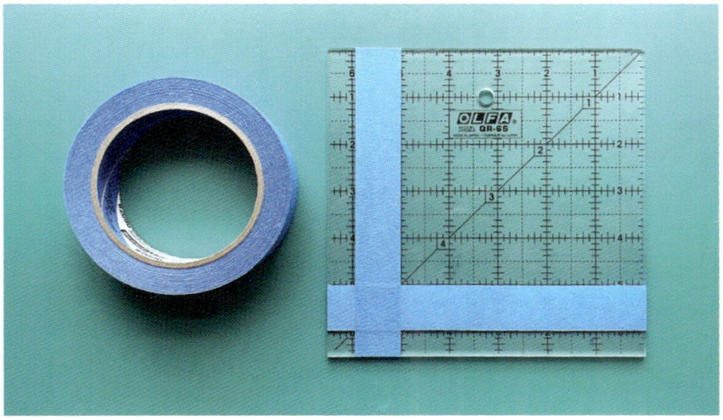

1. Select a ruler that is larger than the block you are cutting. Use painter's tape or washi tape to mark off the measurement you are cutting to. In this example, I am fussy cutting 5½" (14cm) squares, so I placed painter's tape even with the 5½" (14cm) lines of my 6⅕" (15.8cm) ruler.

2. Place the ruler over the motif you are going to cut out. Center the design in the window created by the tape, keeping in mind that the outer ¼ will be absorbed by the seam allowance.

3. Once you are happy with your placement, trim the left and top sides off with a rotary cutter.

4. Turn the fabric 180 degrees so the cut edges are now on the left and bottom sides. Realign the ruler, so the tape is even with the cut edges and trim the remaining two sides to size.

Watch a video tutorial on how to fussy cut your fabric with multiple examples of fussy cut motifs.

Fusing Interfacing

Interfacing comes in many different variations depending on what you are using it for. Whenever I use interfacing in this book, it is to achieve a certain texture, stiffness, or to add extra longevity to the project we are working on.

When you buy interfacing at the store, it is important to get the same kind that is recommended for the project, or your results may be different than the sample. Once you get used to the different kinds of interfacing, you can swap some out. For example, instead of batting in the Carry-On Tote (page 44), you could use fusible foam for a more structured look. You can also swap sew-in interfacing for fusible, but fusible is much easier to work with for bag and home décor sewing projects. When you purchase fusible interfacing, it will come with instructions. Review the sheet, but they all are applied about the same way, so these instructions will work universally.

1. Lay the interfacing with the fusible side up. The fusible side is often shiny or has a bumpy texture created by the glue adhesive.

2. Lay the fabric with the right side up on top of the interfacing. ALWAYS have fabric in between your iron and the fusible interfacing. It is much easier to peel interfacing off your ironing board than it is to scrape glue off your iron if you mix up the fusible side with the regular side.

3. Starting with two corners, align the edges of the fabric with the edge of the interfacing, and fuse it in place by placing an iron over the fabric for a few seconds. Be careful not to let the iron touch the fusible directly.

4. Work across the straight edge in between the two corners, aligning the edges of the fabric and interfacing and fusing the edge and about 1" (2.5cm) of fabric in place.

For the projects in this book, we will use three different types of fusibles.

- **Pellon SF101:** A lightweight woven interfacing typically used in garments to give extra stability. We'll use it on bag linings to give extra durability, while maintaining a nice soft feeling. You can get this in white and black colors. Choose the black version when you are working with darker fabrics.
- **Pellon 809 Decor Bond:** This non-woven fusible interfacing is typically used in décor and bag projects to create a stiffness to the fabric. We'll use it on placemats to give it a more structured look that can withstand washings.
- **Pellon 897F Fusible Fleece:** This woven fusible is exactly what it sounds like, fleece with a fusible applied to one side. We'll use it on inside décor and bag projects to add a little softness that can be quilted through like batting. You won't have to worry about using a minimum quilting distance because the fleece won't separate over time like batting does.

5. Repeat Steps 3 and 4 until all the corners and edges are fused together.

6. Working across the center, fuse the center fabric to the center of the interfacing, being careful not to wrinkle the fabric.

7. Flip the fabric and fusible over so the fusible is facing up. Check for places where the fusible did not adhere to the fabric and repeat the fusing process, if needed.

Note: If you are working with a placemat that is very warped, leave the top edge open when you are working on Step 5. Then, proceed to Step 6 and allow any excess fabric to hang out over the top edge of the interfacing. Trim the fabric to match the interfacing when you are done fusing.

Finishing Your Quilt

Taking the time to prep your finished top and backing, carefully build your quilt sandwich, and to bind cleanly will make all the difference. You spent time creating your beautiful quilt top, don't let the finishing work distract from that.

The Quilt Sandwich

The first time I heard the term "quilt sandwich," I just nodded my head and pretended I knew what it meant. It was one of the strangest terms I'd ever heard! Eventually, I learned it was a term to describe layering the quilt backing, batting, and quilt top. Making your quilt sandwich correctly is very critical to the outcome of your quilt.

PREPPING THE QUILT TOP

Before I layer my quilt top, I carefully press it and then sew a ⅛" (0.32cm) seam around the entire perimeter. The stitching acts like a stay stitch, ensuring that the edges of the quilt stay square and straight before quilting. It also helps hold sewn seams together while quilting.

PREPPING THE BACKING

Choosing your backing fabric is a lot of fun. Backing fabric should always measure 10" (25.40cm) wider than the quilt top to allow for shrinkage as you quilt. After quilting, you will trim any excess. You will piece the backing, or you may find 108" (2.7m) fabric at your quilt shop to accommodate a seamless backing on your quilt. Fabric requirements that include extra fabric for backing are included in the materials lists of the projects in this book.

Choosing a quilt design is as much of a creative decision as choosing your fabrics and pattern design. Whether you choose a simple design or a more intricate one, quilting enhances the design of your project.

To prep your backing fabric, cut off selvages with a rotary cutter. Cut the backing fabric into as many equal widths as you need to span the quilt. With right sides together, sew the widths of fabric together along the cut sides, using a ¼" (6.4mm) seam. Press the seams open and press the backing fabric well.

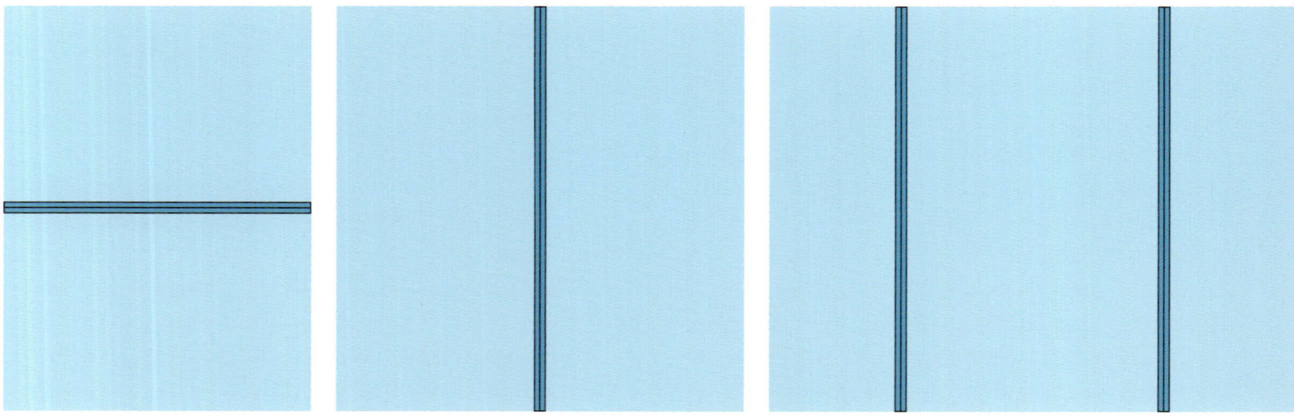

Quilt backing is sewn together from widths of fabric with the seams running either horizontally (left) or vertically (center). Quilts smaller than 74" (187.96cm) on any side will use two widths of fabric sewn together to make the backing. Quilts larger than 74" (187.96cm) will require three widths of fabric (right) sewn together to create a backing large enough to extend 10" (25.4cm) larger than the quilt top.

LAYERING THE QUILT SANDWICH

You will need a large, flat area to lay out your backing, batting, and quilt top; the size of this area depends on the size of your quilt. I created my work surface out of a pair of 6' (1.8m) tables and two sets of plastic bed risers. I placed the tables side by side on top of the risers to raise the tables to counter height. Layers don't have to fit edge to edge on the surface. They can drape evenly off the sides of a table.

Start by laying the backing wrong side up on your work surface and smoothing out any wrinkles. Use tape or binder clips to keep the backing in place.

Layer the bumpy side of the batting, facing up, on the quilt backing. Smooth out any wrinkles. (**Note:** If wrinkles are hard to smooth out, throw the batting in the dryer on low heat with a wet washcloth for a few minutes to reduce wrinkles.) Then, center the quilt top over the backing and batting, making sure to smooth out all three layers as much as possible.

PINNING THE QUILT SANDWICH

If you are quilting on your home sewing machine, I recommend pin-basting because it's the easiest way to keep layers in place. I prefer bent quilting pins to make it easier to rock into and out of the layers. Start in the center of the quilt and pin every 6" (15.25cm), through all three layers. Continue pinning, pulling the draped areas onto the table and smoothing out the layers. (**Note:** If you are using your dining-room table or anything other than a dedicated work surface, take care not to poke pins into the surface.)

Batting Choices

Batting choices play an important role in the outcome of your quilt. I've used all kinds of batting brands and fiber contents over my time as a quilter and have found that Quilter's Dream® is my favorite brand. No matter which fiber content you choose, they are all dense and opaque.

That second part really matters if you want to use a dark backing fabric and have a light background. I found that out the hard way when I sent my husband to the store once to purchase any white batting to highlight the white background I had used on a quilt. He showed up with a loosely bound white polyester batting that was completely see through. That white background I really wanted to stand out ended up looking pink with the solid red backing fabric showing through the batting.

Pellon is a dense, opaque batting option that you can find in big-box stores.

When I'm out of batting and need to grab some from a big-box store, I always go for a dense, opaque option that is as close to Quilter's Dream as possible. The Warm Company® and Pellon® both have battings that you can easily find in big-box stores that have similar qualities.

My first choice is always 100-percent cotton batting, but I find most 80/20 blends quilt in almost the same way and hold up just as nicely. If my background is white, I prefer to use bleached batting. If my background is cream or another color, natural is just fine and a little less expensive. For quilts with dark navy or black backgrounds, a 100-percent black polyester batting adds a very nice touch and ensures you won't get any white fuzzies poking through the backing.

For very special projects where I want the quilting to shine, I will layer a 100-percent polyester on the bottom and a 100-percent wool batting on top. This combination provides a lot of stability and puff. It's great when you really want the details of your quilting to shine. But it does make the quilt rather stiff and not super snuggly. If you want puff but still want a nice drape, then a single layer of 100-percent wool is the way to go.

I have quilted with bamboo, and it is very soft with a wonderful drape, but in a wash and wear test I did for the Quilt Addicts Anonymous YouTube Channel, I found it didn't shrink evenly. The same was true for polyester battings that have a significant amount of puff. The volume tends to break down the more it

Choosing the right thread for your quilt is an important step in the quilt sandwich process.

is washed with the lofty polyester battings, whereas wool will hold its volume and shape as it is washed.

No matter which batting brand or fiber content you choose, it is critically important to know what the required quilting density is for your batting. Some battings recommend you quilt no further than 3" (7.6cm) apart to prevent the batting from shifting and separating over time. That's going to rule out any of those wide-open, all-over meanders and loose outlining of motifs in the center panel.

My preferred 100-percent cotton Quilter's Dream batting allows you to quilt up to 7" (17.8cm) apart. I rarely quilt that loosely, but if you don't want a super dense look, then make sure you choose a batting that will allow you to quilt loosely without compromising the longevity of your quilt.

Thread Choices

When I am working on my home sewing machine, I use Aurifil 50wt cotton thread. It works great for piecing and quilting, and it is buildable, which means you can travel over your previous stitches without making it look too bulky. It also is very low lint, so it means you can go longer in between machine cleanings.

When I'm working on my longarm, I use Glide 40wt polyester thread for the top thread, and I use the pre-wound bobbins in the same weight. I found that my longarm is not a fan of cotton thread, and it doesn't build very nicely. Whereas I can get pretty dense and detailed with the Glide 40wt poly and have beautiful results.

Some long arm models tend to behave best with a certain brand of thread, so you may need to experiment a bit to figure out what works best for yours. You're looking for something that won't break easily, you can set the tension for without too much

Match your thread to the same color as the background of your quilt or one shade lighter.

trouble, and one that just kind of blends into the fabric so the texture you create enhances the quilt design and fabric, without pulling focus to a thick thread, unless that's what you're going for.

Regardless of what thread or sewing machine I am using, I have a few guidelines I tend to follow when it comes to thread color. For straight-line quilting and all over designs, I tend to choose a light-colored thread that will coordinate with all the colors in the quilt. Often, I am choosing a bright white, bone, or light gray, but depending on the quilt, celery green, light pink, light blue, and pale yellow may also work. The best option is to either match the thread to the same color as the background or one shade lighter, or pick a light color that is prominent throughout most of the fabrics used in the quilt if there's not a clear background.

For custom quilting or rulerwork, I will sometimes change threads while quilting. The most basic would be two colors: one color for the background and one color that coordinates with the rest of the fabrics in the quilt. But I have been known to go overboard on the color changes, using up to a dozen threads in one quilt rather than detract from it.

If I am using two or more threads, I will start with the color that will be used most prominently in the quilt. That is usually the background. I'll quilt with that thread from top to bottom on my longarm. Then, I'll switch threads to the next color and quilt from the bottom to the top. I repeat that process as many times as I need to until all the colors are used. On the last pass, I carefully look across the quilt to make sure I've not missed any sections.

Quilting the Quilt

There's absolutely nothing wrong with using a simple all-over meander when you're quilting a panel quilt. It can be an excellent option, especially if you've chosen to create a panel quilt for speed or you're making the quilt for a child, and you expect it to be laundered frequently.

But one of the ways to elevate a panel quilt is to use custom quilting to highlight the aspects of the panel you fell in love with. It's also a great way to practice and improve your free motion quilting skills because you always have a motif to follow. In this section, we'll cover some of the techniques I use to make the panels pop, including thread and batting choice, plus mixing quilting techniques so the non-panel parts can be a little bit more basic to save time and keep the focus where you want it—on the beautiful artwork of the panel.

ALL-OVER DESIGNS AND STENCILS

If you're on a tight deadline, making a donation quilt, or the quilt is going somewhere where it will be laundered often, like to a child, then an all-over free-motion meander might be a good option for you. That doesn't mean you're stuck with a wide-open stipple meander. There are lots of stencils, pantographs, and machine-guided meanders that can customize the quilting to fit the theme and feel of your quilt.

Full Line Stencil is one of my favorite stencil companies.

One of my favorite stencil companies is Full Line Stencil. They offer hundreds of stencil designs on a screen printing-like material. You line the stencil up on your quilt, and use a chalk powder applicator called a Pounce Pad to swipe the chalk through the screen to place the design on your quilt top. When you're done, you can wipe the chalk away.

I love to use these when the design I want to make is a little more complicated than I feel like I can do freehand, or when I want to have a special treatment. For example, I used a feather border stencil in the center of my 7" (17.8cm) border for Alternating Stars Owl Quilt (page 104). Then, I filled in around the stencil freehand to create a custom look.

Pantographs can be a nice option for longarm quilters. They work by placing the panto on the

Longarm quilters often use pantographs.

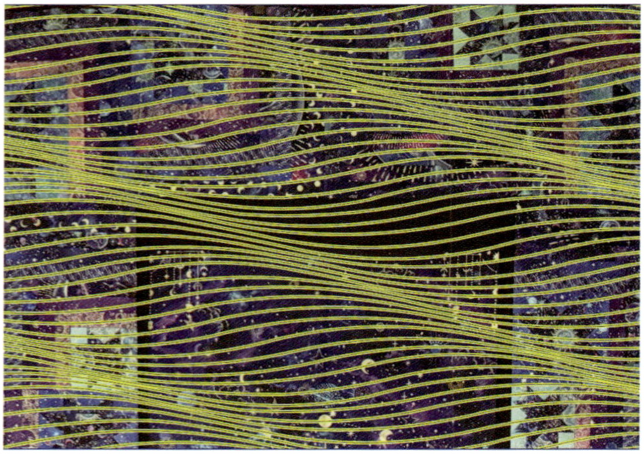

You can work with a longarmer to use a computerized system for stitching.

machine quilting frame behind the quilt and following the lines on the design with a laser attached to your machine. You're not actually looking at the quilt when you are stitching, you are watching the pantograph lines. It's a great way to get a custom all-over meander without having to mark your quilt.

Another option is to work with a longarmer who has a computerized system for their longarm. There are thousands of computerized quilting stitches to choose from to match the theme and feel of your quilt. Whether you are using a computerized stitch on your own longarm or working with a professional, take the time to ensure the stitch size is customized to work with your quilt.

For example, all the designs in this book where the panel is meant to be used intact are designed to be used with 12" (30.5cm) finished blocks. If you choose a 9-patch block, the finished pieces of your block will be 4" (10.2cm) square, so the meander should be sized to fit nicely within those 4" (10.2cm).

But, if you chose a 16-patch block, then the finished pieces of your block will be 3" (7.6cm) square, so the meander should be sized down appropriately for the scale of the design to match the scale of your smaller pieces. This little bit of attention to detail makes a big difference between an average-looking quilt and one that looks custom, even though you're using an all-over stitch.

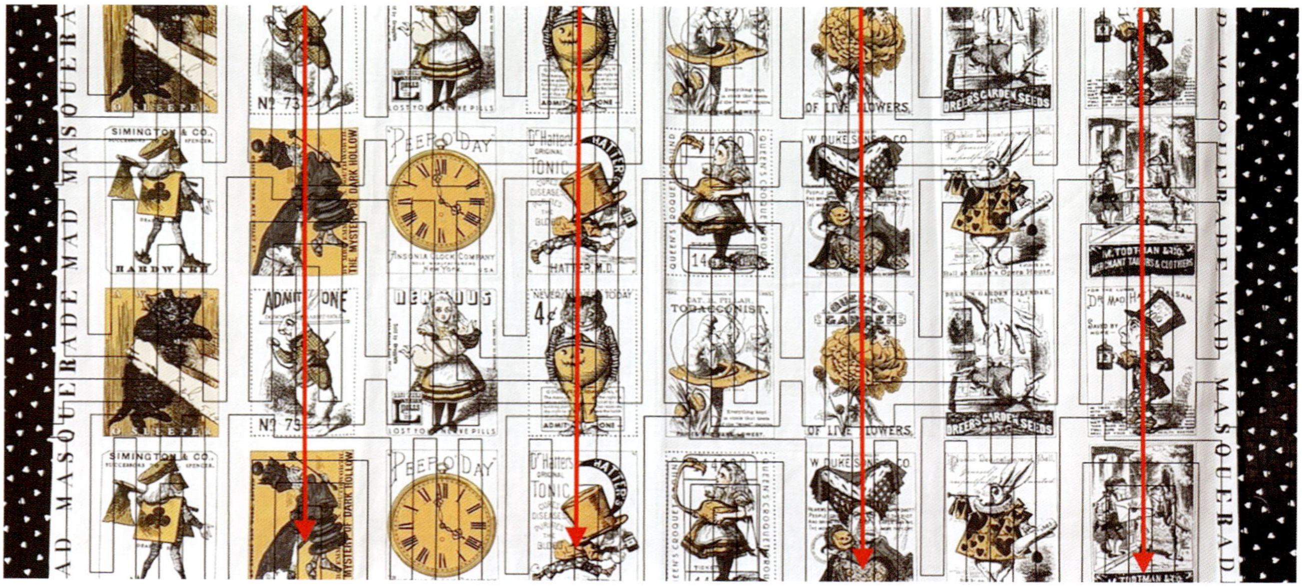

SHELLY MOORE

SHELLY MOORE

STRAIGHT-LINE QUILTING

Another perfectly acceptable option of quilting is straight-line quilting. This can be done on a longarm with a ruler or channel locks, or on a domestic sewing machine with a walking foot. Just about every quilt I made at the beginning of my quilting life was done with straight-line walking foot quilting because that was all I knew how to do and could look reasonably nice on my first sewing machine.

I used straight-line quilting for this pillow.

I still use straight-line quilting when the pattern is ultra-modern, or in home décor projects. The pillow, table runner, and placemat designs in this book look fabulous with straight lines quilted at 1" (2.5cm) intervals or stitch-in-the ditch, where you quilt in or just next to the seam. Both are very easy to accomplish on your home sewing machine, so you can have a quick finish that doesn't involve a longarm.

CUSTOM QUILTING

My favorite way to quilt a panel is with custom quilting. I love to take the design of the artwork as my guide and bring it to life with outlined stitches. You can get as detailed as you want with this step, either going loosely around just the main elements with a single thread color, or densely quilting each figure with coordinating thread, even using decorative thread choices to add shine and sparkle. Some quilters will even add Swarovski crystals to the final quilt to make details pop.

I tend to end up somewhere in the middle. For quilts that will be used on beds and as couch throws, I quilt around the details in a medium-density design, using the lines of the drawing as my guide. I find it is not unlike following the lines of a quilting stencil, so

Custom quilting is my favorite way to quilt panels.

When quilting a wall hanging, you can add elements to make your project stand out that you can't use with a blanket.

if you can do that easily, then you are ready to follow around a motif as well.

Background can be a bit trickier. If there aren't a lot of cues from fabric design, you might want to try a free-motion stitch that makes sense in the space, such as ripples for water, clouds in the sky, or swirls in a snowy landscape. Sometimes I'll change thread colors, or I'll go with one that works with everything. I let the fabric be my guide.

For projects that aren't going to be snuggled with, such as a wall hanging, I make different choices to ensure my quilting really stands out. Instead of the typical single layer of 100-percent cotton batting, I choose a double batting of a polyester bottom and wool top. The combination makes for a stiff finish that will help your wall hanging stay straight, and the double batting with wool on top will really make your quilting details pop.

There are so many options here that it could warrant their own books. But use your panel projects as an opportunity to play and really experiment with what you are capable of when it comes to free-motion quilting. Start by outlining the main features of the panel design, then see what you can do. Create texture in clothing, add wood-grain stitches over trees, and quilt the background tight and dense and the figures looser to create a three-dimensional effect. Your imagination is your only limit. Push yourself and see what you can create.

Binding the Quilt

Binding is the piece of fabric that wraps around the raw edges of your quilt to hide the batting and secure the edges of your quilt. I always write my patterns to include 2½" (6.40cm) binding. My preferred method of sewing binding is the continuous method, so that you can't tell where the binding strip starts and stops. It makes a nice, smooth finish around all the edges. Joining the ends can be a little intimidating at first, but once you do it, you'll never want to go back to methods that tuck the strip and create a lump. "The Quilt Addicts Anonymous Beginner Quilting" series includes a free video that shows you each of the steps explained in this section.

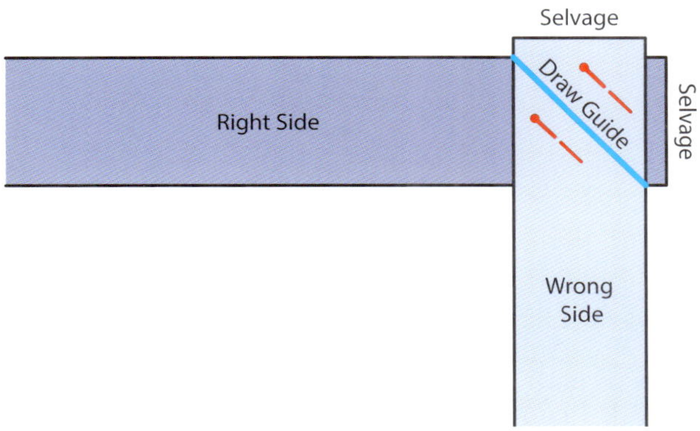

1. Arrange your binding strips right sides together at a right angle so that the horizontal strip is right side up, and the vertical strip is right side down. Allow the selvages to hang past the edges of the strips. This will create two valleys that you will sew between. Pin the strips in place. Draw a line from valley to valley from the top left to the bottom right.

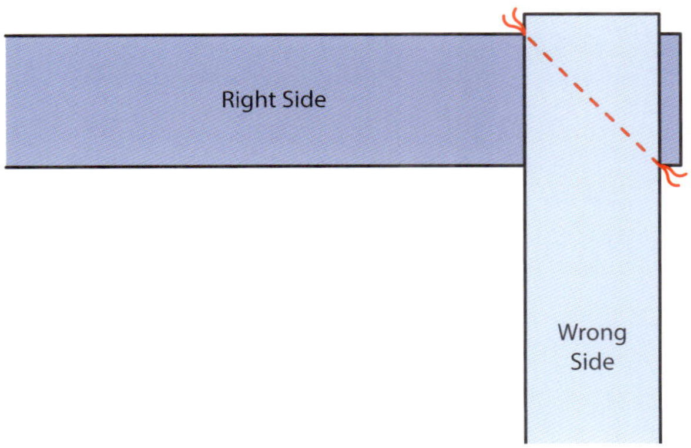

2. Sew on the line, removing the pins before you sew over them.

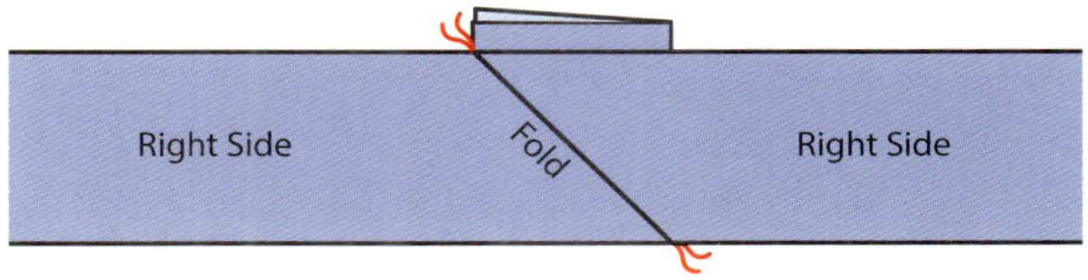

3. Open your strip to make sure the two strips make a straight line.

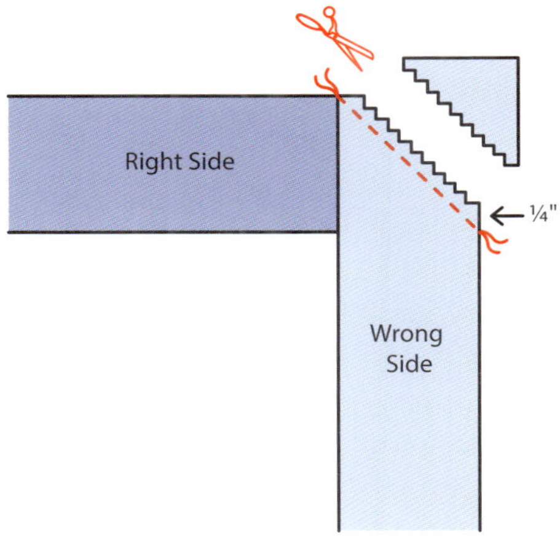

4. Trim the corner off to create a ¼" (6.4mm) seam. Repeat until all your binding strips are sewn together.

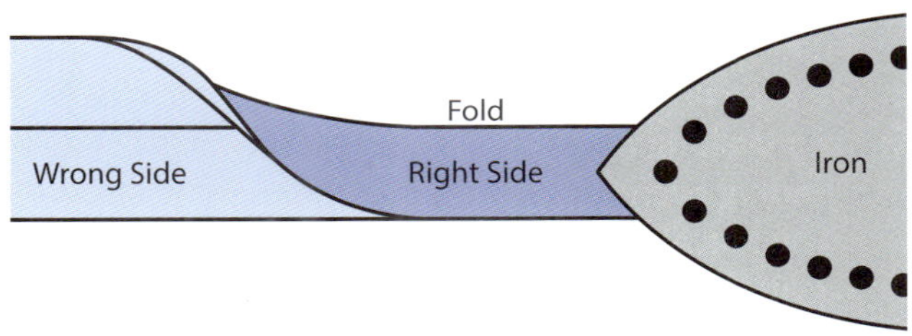

5. Fold the binding in half with the long sides together and press in place. Press diagonal seams to the side as you come to them.

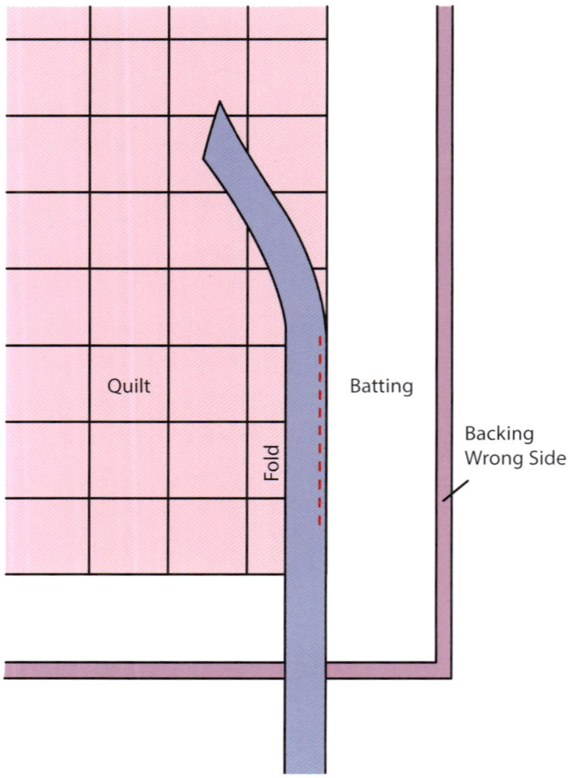

6. Starting on the bottom of your quilt, lay your binding even with the edge of your quilt top. Leave about 6" (15.24cm) free, and start sewing the binding to the edge of your quilt top through all three layers using a walking foot, always keeping the edges of the binding even with the edge of the quilt top. I also use Machingers® Quilting Gloves at this step to help grip the fabric and move the quilt through the machine easily.

7. Stop with your needle down when you are ¼" (6.4mm) away from the edge of the first corner. Lift your presser foot and turn the quilt, so the next edge is now facing you. Lift your needle up, and gently pull the quilt out from under the presser foot a couple of inches (about 5cm).

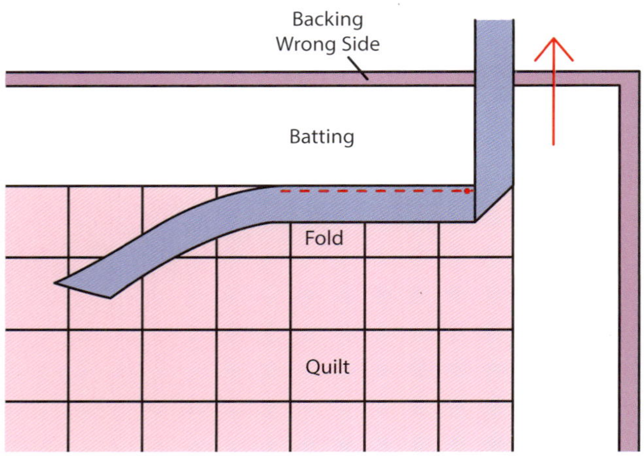

8. Fold the binding back so that the raw edges are even with the side of the quilt top, and the fold makes a 45-degree angle directly into the corner of the quilt.

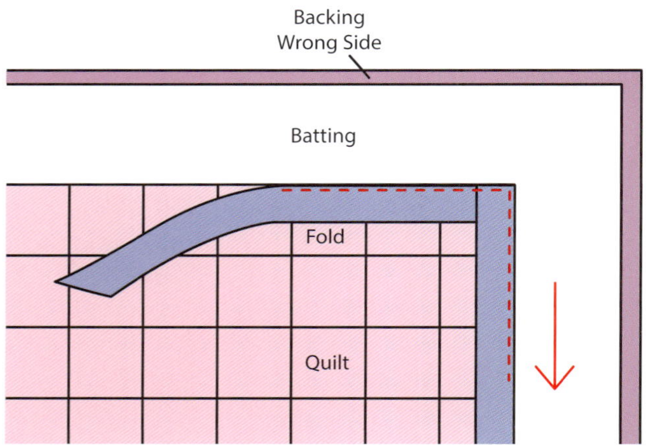

9. Fold the binding down so that the raw edges are even with the edges of the quilt top, and there is a triangle flap at the corner that you will turn over and stitch down later to create a mitered corner.

10. Continue sewing, repeating the mitered corner steps for the remaining three corners. Stop sewing about 12" (30.48cm) before the point where you started sewing. Break your thread, and remove the quilt from the sewing machine.

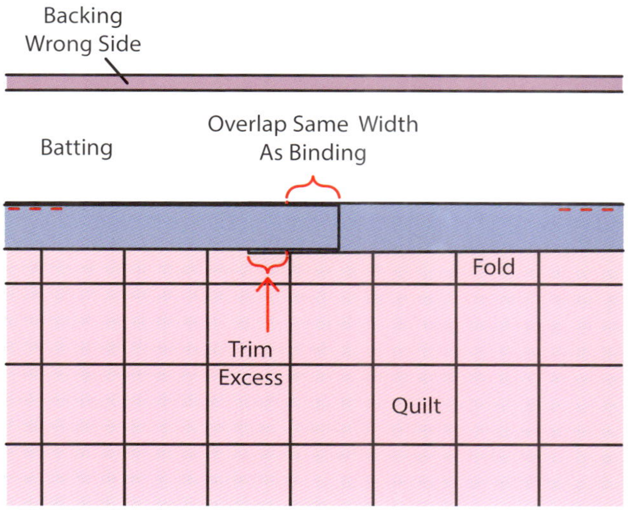

11. Select the beginning of the binding, and trim it square in the center of the open section of binding. This should be about 6" (15.24cm) in between where the binding starts and stops. Lay the quilt flat on a table, and arrange the trimmed binding piece flat against it with the raw edges of the binding even with the edges of the quilt top. Lay a ruler even with the trimmed edge of the binding. Now lay the end of the binding over the beginning of the binding, keeping the raw edges even with the edges of the quilt. Trim the binding end so that it overlaps exactly 2½" (6.35cm) past the beginning of the binding.

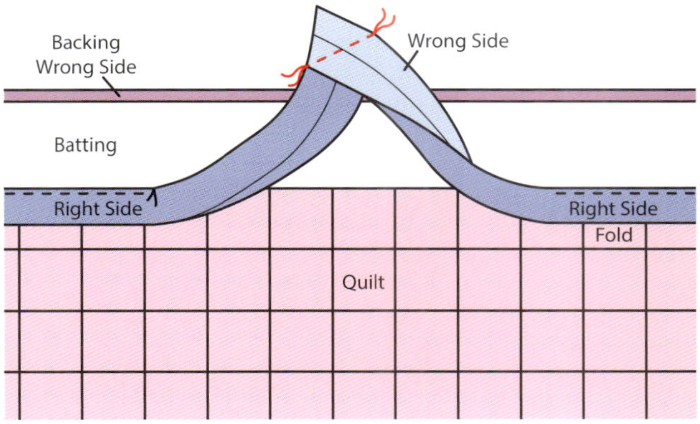

12. Arrange the binding edges perpendicular to each other like you did when you were first sewing the binding strips together, except now the edges will lines up exactly. Pin them in place and draw a line from the corners of the binding, so you have a guide to sew on. Sew the binding together, removing the pins before you sew over them.

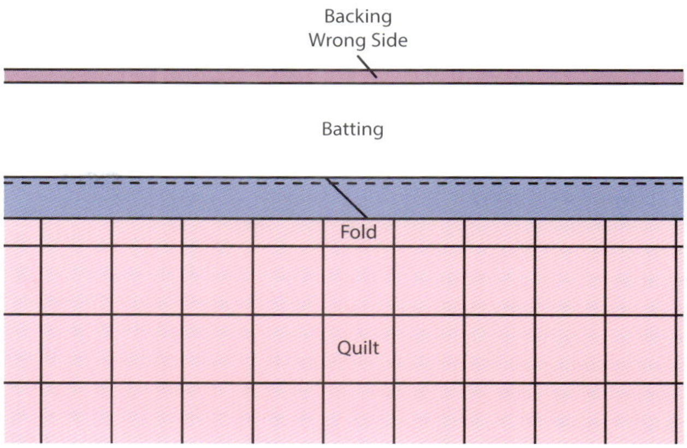

13. Lay the quilt back on a flat table, and test to make sure the binding lies flat against the quilt top with no excess fabric or tightness. Once you are satisfied, trim the seam to ¼" (6.4mm), and sew the binding to the quilt top through all three layers.

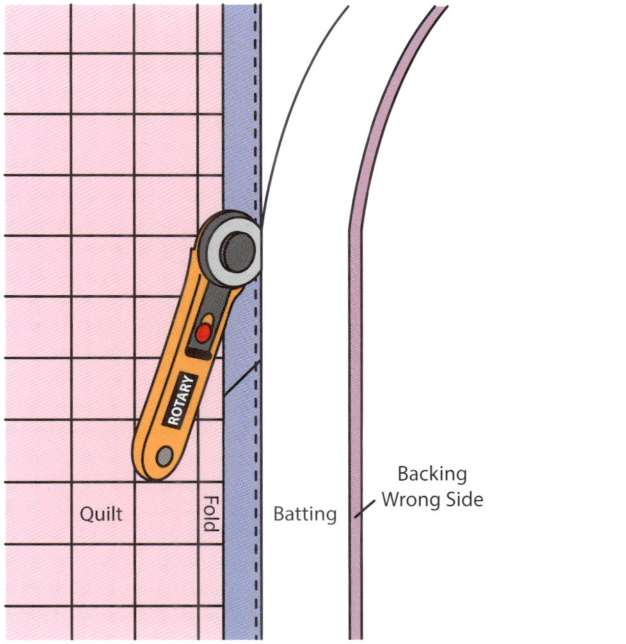

14. Trim the excess batting off so that the batting and backing are now even with the quilt top. When trimming the mitered corners, be careful that you don't accidentally slice the binding.

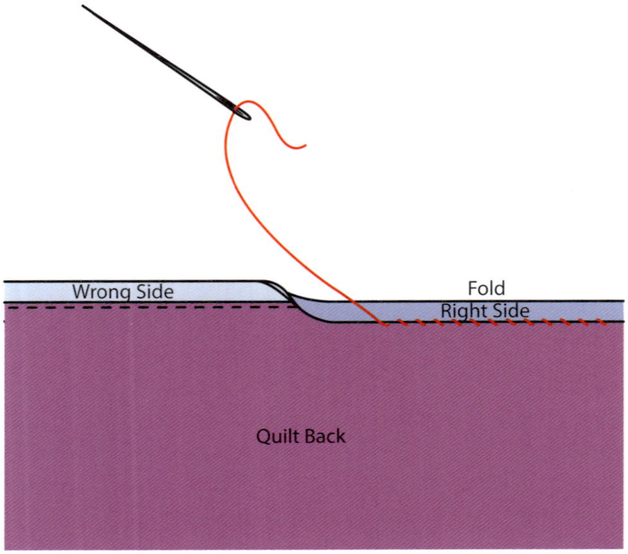

15. Fold the binding around to the back of the quilt. The binding should fit snugly around the edges of the quilt; there should be neither a gap between the edge of the batting and the edge of the binding nor a bump where the batting is folded back because the binding is folded too far. Knot your thread, and insert your needle about 1" (2.54cm) from the edge of your binding, going through the quilt back and batting but not the top. Bring the needle out on the fold of the binding. Give your thread a tug to bury the knot in between the quilt layers. Blind stitch until you reach the corner of the quilt.

TIP

Binding clips and thread that matches your binding fabric can make binding much easier when you are just getting started.

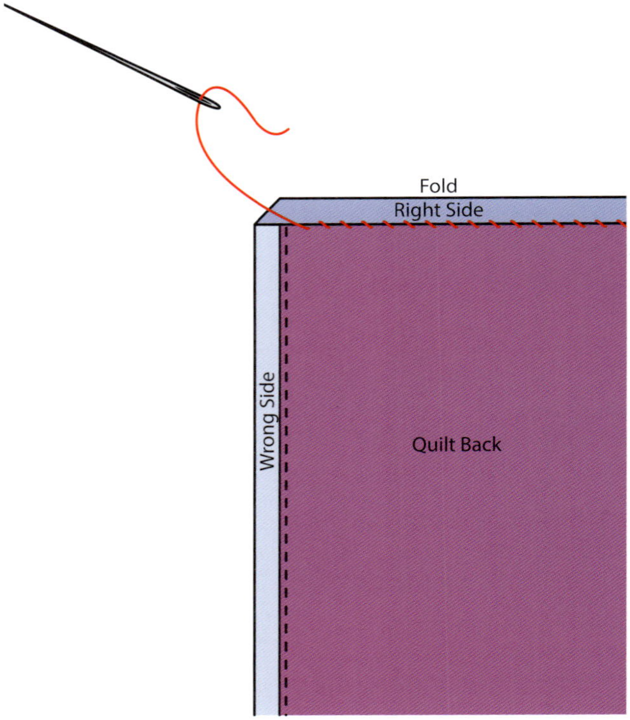

16. Once you have sewed all the way to the corner, use your needle to travel to the front corner of the quilt, bringing your needle out right where the binding makes a 45-degree fold on the front of your quilt. Travel to the corner of your quilt, tacking the top edge of the binding in place. Insert your needle through the 45-degree fold, coming out in the back corner of the quilt. Fold the next binding edge down so that it makes a 45-dgree angle and meets the edge of the edge you just finished sewing. Take two or three stitches down the 45-degree fold, tacking it down. Take one extra stitch at the bottom of the 45-degree fold, and then continue with the blind stitch and mitered corners until the binding is complete.

Panel Projects

Enjoy this collection of panel projects designed to encourage you to think beyond just making a simple quilt. Of course, I've included some designs in that category, but you'll also find pillows, totes, placemats, a runner, wall hangings, and even a playmat. Panels offer so much more creative potential. And don't forget, if you need a little additional help, just scan the QR code with each pattern to watch the free tutorial online.

Quilted Panel Throw Pillows
(With Invisible Zipper)

Finished Size: 18" (45.7cm)

When you see a panel you love, it doesn't just have to be turned into a quilt. Throw pillows can be a fun, easy way to showcase the panel designs and coordinating fabrics in the collection. They can also be a great way to use a new collection from a designer you love. Then, you can style the pillows with previous quilts you've made, like I've done here with Earth Song by Laurel Burch.

I have an entire shelf in my quilt collection dedicated to Laurel Burch quilts I've made over the years collaborating with Clothworks Fabrics. This was the perfect opportunity to create a cohesive scene in my home by pairing the quilted throw pillows with my Charm Squared pattern using Laurel Burch basics.

When you are hunting for panels, keep in mind that the panel doesn't have to exactly fit the specifications in the pattern. The original panel for this project featured four large vertical rectangles of jungle animals, plus a fun border print. I chose my two favorite animals and fussy cut two 10½" (26.7cm) squares. The rest is in my stash waiting for a future project.

One final note: while zippers may seem intimidating, I've broken it down here to be as easy as possible. Plus, you can follow along with a video tutorial. Throw pillow covers are a lot easier to store than throw pillows, so you can easily switch up the look of your living room and bedding to match each season without taking up tons of closet space.

Fabric Requirements

Panel	Background	Pillow Front	Pillow Back	Fusible Fleece	Pillow Forms	Zippers
(1) 24" x 44" (61 x 111.7cm)	½ yard (45.72cm)	Corners: ½ yard (45.72cm)	8 fat eighths	2¼ yards (205.74cm)	(2) 18" (45.7cm) pillow forms	(2) 22" (55.9cm) invisible zippers
		Long rectangles: fat quarter				

Watch a video tutorial on how to piece the pillow front and back!

Cutting Instructions

PANEL: FRONT

1. Fussy cut two 10½" (26.7cm) squares.

PILLOW CORNERS: FRONT

2. Fussy cut eight 5" (12.7cm) squares from the panel or motifs from a coordinating fabric for the pillow front corners.

FAT QUARTER: FRONT

3. Cut four 4" x 21" (10.2cm x 53.3cm) strips, crosscut into 4" x 10½" (10.2 x 26.7cm) strips.

BACKGROUND: FRONT AND BACK

4. Cut four 1½" (3.8cm) x WOF strips. Cross cut into eight 1½" x 10½" (3.8 x 26.7cm) strips for the pillow front.

5. Cut three 1½" (3.8cm) x WOF strips. Cross cut into six 1½" x 19" (3.8 x 48.3cm) strips for the pillow back.

6. Cut two 1¾" (4.5cm) x WOF strips. Cross cut the strips into four 1¾" (4.5cm) x WOF strips for the pillow back.

FAT EIGHTHS: BACK

7. From each fat eighth, cut one 3¾" x 21" (9.5 x 53.3cm) strips from eight fabrics. Cut four strips into a 3¾" x 4¾" (9.5 x 12.1cm) rectangle and a 3¾" x 14¾" (9.5 x 37.46cm) rectangle. Cut four strips into two 3¾" x 10" (9.5 x 25.4cm) rectangles.

FUSIBLE FLEECE

8. Cut two 19" (48.3cm) x WOF strips of fusible fleece, crosscut into four 19" (48.3cm) squares of fusible fleece.

9. Cut two 18" (45.7cm) x WOF strips of fusible fleece, crosscut into four 19" (48.3cm) squares of fusible fleece.

Quilt Throw Pillow Assembly

ASSEMBLING THE PILLOW FRONT

This portion of the project is sewn using a ¼" (6.4mm) seam allowance.

1. Select the eight 4" x 10½" (10.2 x 26.7cm) fat quarter strips and the eight 1½" x 10½" (3.8 x 26.7cm) (background strips. Arrange as shown above.

2. With the right sides together, sew the fat quarter strips to the background strips. Press the seams open.

3. Select the fussy cut 5" (12.7cm) pillow corners and the fussy cut 10½" (26.7cm) panel squares. Arrange as shown above with the pieced units from step 2. You have enough pieces to make two pillow fronts.

4. Join the pillow front pieces into horizontal rows. Press the seams open.

5. Join the horizontal rows to complete the pillow top. Press the seams open. You should have two pillow fronts measuring 19" (48.3cm) square.

ASSEMBLING THE PILLOW BACK

This portion of the project is sewn using a ¼" (6.4mm) seam allowance.

1. For each pillow and using assorted prints, select two 3¾" x 4¾" (9.5 x 12.1cm) rectangles, two 3¾" x 14¾" (9.5 x 37.46cm) rectangles, and four 3¾" x 10" (9.5 x 25.4cm) rectangles. For each pillow, you will also need three 1½" x 19" (3.8 x 48.3cm) background strips for the center sashing and two 1¾" x 19" (4.5 x 48.3cm) strips for the top and bottom sashing. Arrange all as shown above.

2. With the right sides together, join the 3¾" x 4¾" (9.5 x 12.1cm) rectangles and 3¾" x 14¾" (9.5 x 37.46cm) rectangles together to create two rows. Also, join the 3¾" x 10" (9.5 x 25.4cm) rectangles to create two rows. Press all seams open.

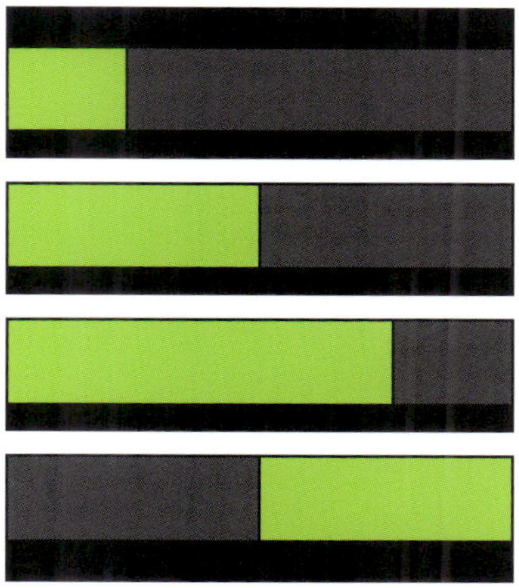

3. Sew the rows to the background sashing strips, making sure to sew the two 1¾" x 19" (4.5 x 48.3cm) strips for the top and bottom of the pillow. You should have two pillow backs measuring 19" (48.3cm) square.

APPLYING THE FUSIBLE FLEECE

You're going to use two layers of fusible fleece on your pillows instead of quilt batting. This will provide good structure for the throw pillow, while keeping it soft and comfortable. Fusible fleece also doesn't have a minimum quilting distance, so you can quilt it as much or as little as you want to.

We cut our fusible fleece to two different sizes. One is the size of the pillow front and back when it has been pieced together. The second size is the finished size of the pillow. The two layers are what provides a store-bought structure to the pillow, and the two sizes will help to eliminate bulk in the seams, making it easier to assemble.

Watch a video tutorial on how to apply the fusible fleece.

1. With the bumpy, fusible side of the 19" (48.3cm) square fusible fleece facing up, place the pillow front with the right side facing up. Fuse the corners first, followed by the sides, then the center, making sure the edges of your pieced front and back are even with the edges of the 19" (48.3cm) fusible fleece. If they are not the same size, you may have had issues piecing or have accidentally grabbed the 18" (45.7cm) square piece of fusible fleece. Using a steam iron or spritzing your pillow front with water before fusing will make the process easier.

2. Repeat this process with the second pillow front and both pillow backs.

3. Flip the pillow front over. Center the 18" (45.7cm) square fusible fleece with the fusible side facing the wrong side of the pillow front. There should be a ½" (1.3cm) from the edges of the 18" (45.7cm) square piece of fusible fleece to the edge of the pillow front. Holding the 18" (45.7cm) square piece of fusible fleece in place, flip the pillow front over and fuse the 18" (45.7cm) square piece in place. A steam iron or spritzing your pillow before fusing is also helpful here.

4. Repeat this process with the second pillow front and both pillow backs.

5. Quilt the two pillow fronts and backs as desired. I used straight-line quilting using a walking foot on my home sewing machine.

CREATING THE PILLOW

This portion of the project is sewn using a ½" (1.3cm) seam allowance and a walking foot.

Watch a video tutorial on how to install an invisible zipper and assemble your pillow.

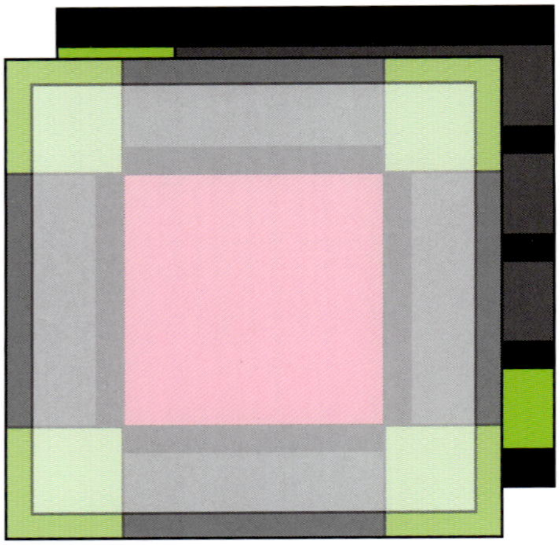

1. Place the pillow front and pillow back right sides together. Make sure directional fabric is pointing the same way.

2. Set your machine to a 2.5 stitch length, backstitch when you begin sewing, then again 2" (5.1cm) from the first corner, indicated by the thick red line. Increase your stitch length to a 5.0 basting stitch, indicated by the thin red line. Continue sewing until you are 2" (5.1cm) from the second corner. Reduce your stitch length to 2.5 again, backstitch, sew to the end of the side, and backstitch. This has created our pillow bottom where our zipper will go. Once the zipper is installed, we will remove the basting stitches so we can slip the pillow inside.

3. Press the seam open.

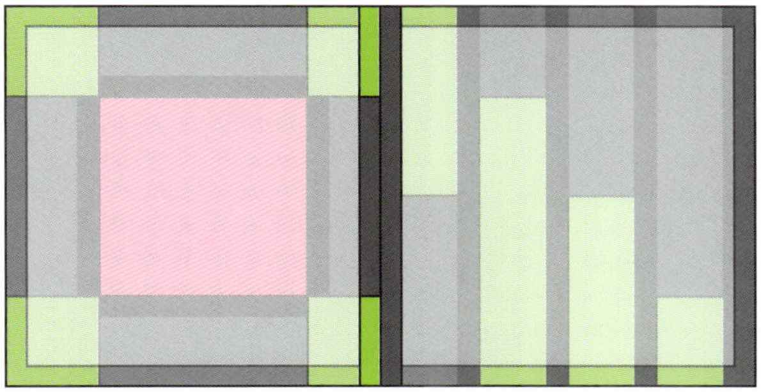

4. Place the invisible zipper teeth side down directly over the seam. Sew down one side of the zipper tape. Move the zipper pull, so it is over the basting stitches and sew down the second side of the zipper table. Make sure to catch the bottom seam when you are sewing the zipper tape in place.

5. Using a seam ripper, carefully remove the basting stitches, making sure to stop before you reach the backstitching 2" (5.1cm) from each corner. Open the zipper to make sure it works, and create a hole for turning.

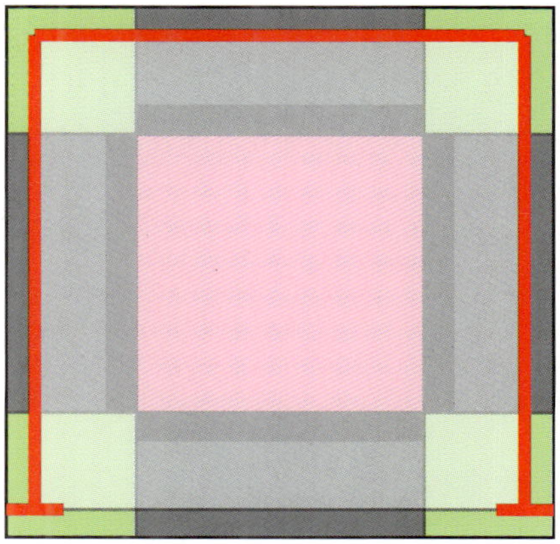

6. Using a 2.5 stitch length, sew around the remaining three sides of the pillow, backstitching at the beginning and end of each seam. You can and should sew over the zipper teeth, just go slowly.

7. Trim the zipper tape even with the edges of the pillow, and turn it right side out to reveal your 18" (45.7cm) throw pillow cover.

8. Repeat steps 1–8 with the second throw pillow cover.

PRO TIP

Professional decorators will stuff extra fiberfill into the corners of a throw pillow cover to make sure it is completely filled out. I did that with my samples.

Halloween Treat Bag

Finished Size: 13" x 16" x 3" (33 x 40.6 x 7.6cm) with 12" (30.5cm) handle drop

The panel tote bag is a great way to use a panel in a nontraditional way, but still be able to show off your favorite prints. The entire project can be made in about two hours, so you can make one for every season, or as gifts for your family and friends. This project works both with horizontal and vertical panels that are 24" (61cm) x WOF, and it will look best if there are two distinct scenes on the panel—one for the front of the tote and one for the back.

The panel tote bag is 13" (33cm) wide, 16" (40.6cm) tall, and 3" (7.6cm) deep, with a 12" (30.5cm) handle drop, so you'll be able to use most of the panel design and fit loads of goodies in yours. Mine will be packed with a laptop, copious kid's snacks, and a hand project for all the time I spend running kids around . . . or an obscene amount of candy during trick or treat.

Fabric Requirements

Panel	Handles	Lining	Fusible Fleece	Pellon SF101
(1) 24" x 44" (61 x 111.7cm)	¼ yard (22.86cm)	⅔ yard (60.96cm)	¾ yard (68.58cm)	1 yard (91.44cm)

Cutting Instructions

PANEL

1. Fussy cut two 17" (43.2cm) wide x 20" (50.8cm) pieces for the front and back tote exterior.

HANDLES

2. Cut two 4" (10.2cm) x WOF strips. Cross cut into two 4" x 30" (10.2 x 76.2cm) strips.

LINING

3. Cut two 17" (43.2cm) wide x 20" (50.8cm) tall pieces.

FUSIBLE FLEECE

4. Cut two 17"(43.2cm) wide x 20" (50.8cm) tall pieces for the tote exterior.

5. Cut two 4" (10.2cm) x WOF strips. Cross cut into two 4" x 30" (10.2 x 76.2cm) strips for the tote handles.

PELLON SF101

6. Cut two 17" (43.2cm) wide x 20" (50.8cm) tall pieces for the tote lining.

PANEL PREPARATION TIP

When you trim the panel to size, keep in mind that the outer 2" (5.1cm) will not be visible from the front or back of the tote. So, keep all the elements of the design you want to see out of the exterior 2" (5.1cm). The top 2" (5.1cm) will be turned under for the tote top hem. The 2" (5.1cm) on sides will be part of the seam allowance and tote side, and the 2" (5.1cm) on the bottom will be part of the seam allowance and tote bottom.

BOO

Panel Tote Assembly

This pattern uses a walking foot for all sewing steps and a ½" (1.3cm) seam allowance.

1. Lay one 17" (43.2cm) wide x 20" (50.8cm) tall piece of fusible fleece with the fusible side up on your ironing surface. Place the 17" (43.2cm) wide x 20" (50.8cm) tall front tote exterior panel piece right side up on top of the fusible fleece, matching the corners and sides of the fabric with the fusible fleece. Follow the manufacturer's instructions to fuse the fleece to the tote exterior panel. Repeat with the second piece of fusible fleece and the back tote exterior panel piece.

2. Use the same technique as step 1 to fuse the two pieces of 17" (43.2cm) wide x 20" (50.8cm) tall Pellon SF101 to the wrong side of the 17" (43.2cm) wide x 20" (50.8cm) tall lining pieces.

3. Identify the top of each of the tote exteriors and place them right sides together, pinning or clipping the sides and bottom together. Sew a ½" (1.3cm) seam around the sides and bottom of the tote, back stitching at the beginning and end of each side. The tote top will be left open.

Step 1

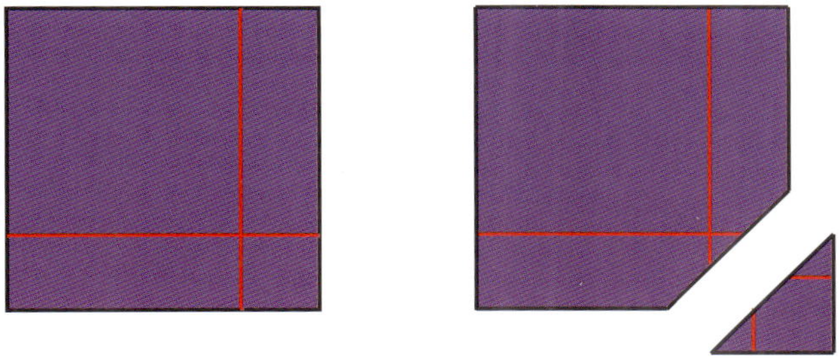

4. Clip the bottom corners of the tote exterior to remove bulk. Be careful not to cut through the seams.

5. Repeat steps 3 and 4 with the tote lining pieces.

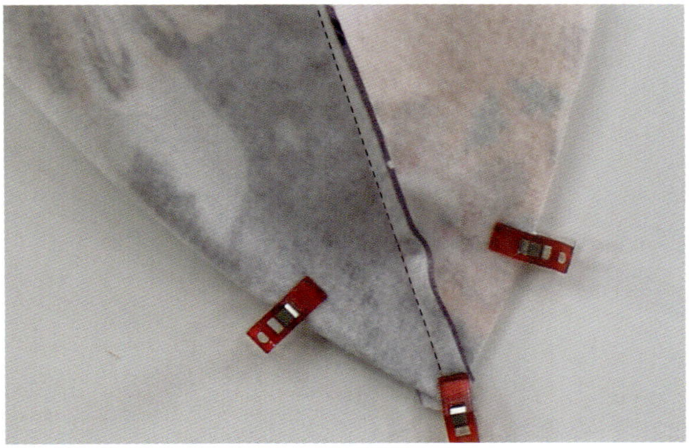

6. Bag Bottom: Select the tote exterior and manipulate the corner, so the seams nest and tote sides form a right angle. Use clips to hold the nesting seams in place. Measure ½" (1.3cm) from the corner seam, and make a mark on the wrong side of the fabric to indicate the distance. Line up a 1" (2.5cm) line of the quilting ruler with the seam and the edge of the ruler with the mark, and draw a line across the wrong side of the tote exterior corner.

7. Sew across the drawn line two to three times, back stitching at the beginning and end of the seam.

8. Repeat steps 6 and 7 with the second corner on the tote exterior and both corners of the tote lining, making sure to keep the bottom seam pressed in the same direction for both corners.

9. Turn the tote exterior right side out, and insert the tote lining inside. The wrong sides should be facing. Pin or clip at the tote side seams, making sure the seams are nested, and across the front and back tote top. Use a ¼" (6.4mm) stitch to baste the tote tops together.

10. Set the tote body to the side, and select the two pieces of 4" x 30" (10.2 x 76.2cm) handle fabric strips and two pieces of the 4" x 30" (10.2 x 76.2cm) fusible fleece. Apply the fusible interfacing to the wrong side of the handles using the same technique as step 1.

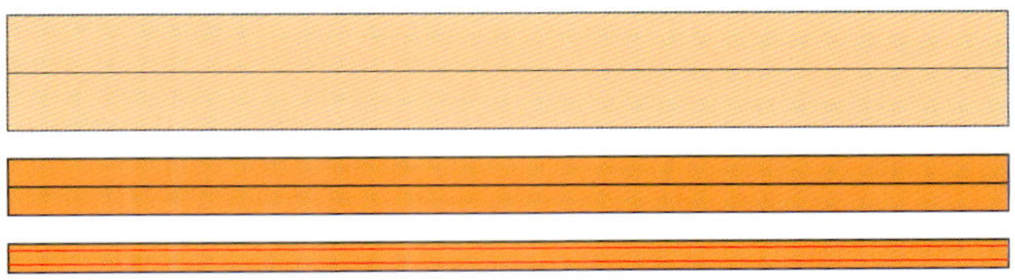

11. Press the handles in half, matching the long sides. Then, press the long edges into the center fold on both long sides, clipping the double-folded sides in place as you press.

12. Stitch close to the edges of the handles on the long sides, starting with the double-fold side.

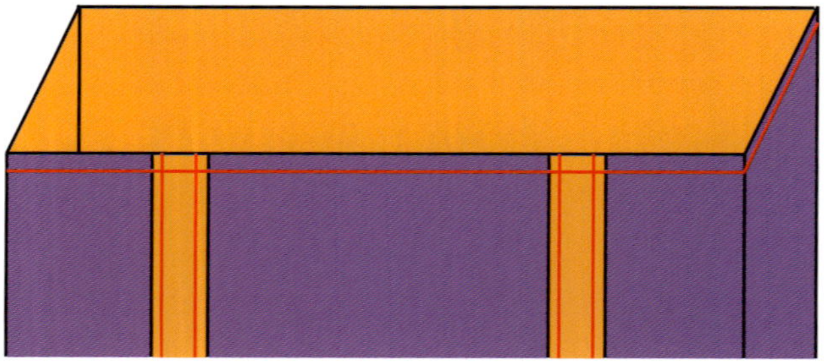

13. Find the center of each bag front and back, and measure 3" (7.6cm) from either side. Place the double-fold side of the handles even with the marked line and clip in place. Repeat on other side of the tote, making sure not to twist the handles. Baste the handle in place.

14. Prepare a double-fold 2" (5.1cm) hem along the top of the tote, and secure it in place with clips, making sure the handles are extending out from the tote top at a 90-degree angle.

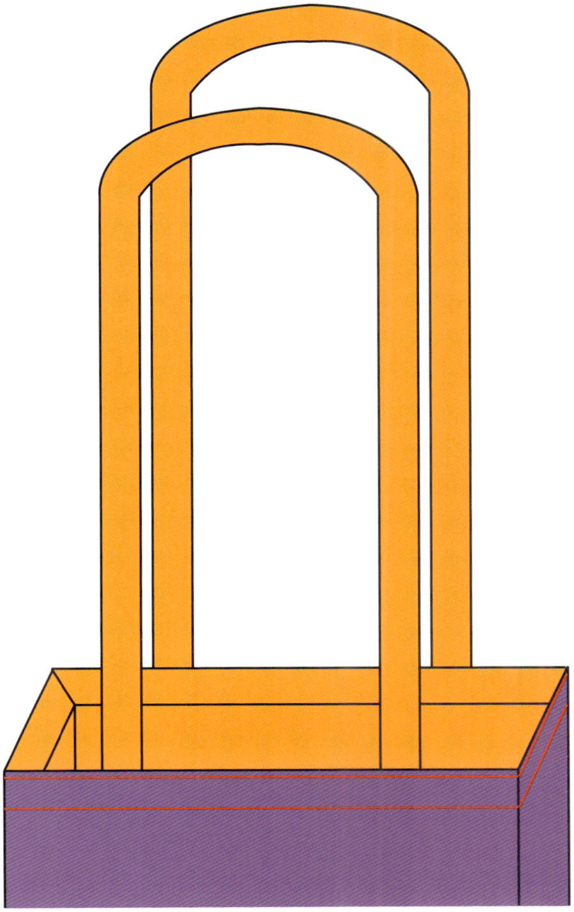

15. Stitch around the top of the tote twice ¾" (1.9cm) from the tote top, back stitching at the beginning and end of the topstitching. Repeat, this time ¼" (6.4mm) from the tote top.

16. Enjoy your tote!

Watch me assemble this tote, including planning where to fussy cut!

Carry-On Tote

Finished Size: 22" x 10" x 9" (55.9 x 25.4 x 22.9cm)

The Carry-On Tote is one of my favorite projects of the entire book. This quilted bag is designed to fit the carry-on requirements for TSA and has a luggage strap on the back, so you can easily slide it on top of your suitcase or sewing machine traveling case handle to bring it with you on your next trip. The design is very similar to a very popular designer quilted carry-on-duffle bag, so you might have your friends asking where you got it. The ends have easy-to-create pockets, and the interior features a mesh four-pocket storage compartment for easy organization.

This project came entirely from my stash using a panel that was designed from an original watercolor painting by Shell Rummel for her Time and Tide for FreeSpirit Fabrics. Shell and I have been frequent collaborators for years, and I had been saving this panel for something special. I paired it with durable shot cotton I had left over from a quilting project for the end panels, pockets, and handles, and I love how it looks with the moody blues of the panel design.

Fabric Requirements

Panel	Pockets/Luggage Strap/Handle	Lining	Backing	Batting	Pellon SF101	Mesh	FOE
(1) 24" x 44" (61 x 111.7cm)	1½ yards (1.4m)	1¼ yards (1.1m)	1¾ yards (1.6m)	1¼ yards (1.1m) of 90" (2.3m) wide batting	1¾ yards (1.1m)	¼ yard (22.86cm)	1¾ yards (1.6m)

Cutting Instructions

PANEL

1. Leave at full size until after quilting. After the panel has been quilted, trim to 23" x 39" (58.4cm x 99.1cm) for the bag body.

POCKETS/LUGGAGE STRAP/ HANDLE

2. Cut a 24" (61cm) x WOF section of fabric for quilting. Once it has been quilted, cut the pieces for steps 3–6.

3. End panels: Cut two 11" (28cm) wide x 10" (25.4cm) tall rectangles.

4. Fold over pocket: Cut two 11" (28cm) wide x 15" (38.1cm) tall rectangles.

5. Luggage strap: Cut one 10" x 13" (25.4 x 33cm) rectangle.

6. Cut four 6" (15.2cm) x WOF sections for the handles; this section is not quilted.

LINING

7. Bag body: Cut one 23" x 39" (58.4 x 99.1cm) rectangle.

8. End panels: Cut two 11" (28cm) wide x 10" (25.4cm) tall rectangles.

9. Cut one fat quarter for bias binding.

BACKING

10. Cut two 28" (71.12cm) x WOF strips to use as backing for the panel and pockets/luggage strap backing.

BATTING

11. Panel and pockets/luggage strap: Cut two 28" x 44" (71.2 x 111.7cm) rectangles.

12. Handles: Cut two 6" x 80" (15.2 x 203.2cm) strips.

PELLON SF101

13. End panels: Cut two 11" (28cm) wide x 10" (25.4cm) tall rectangles.

14. Bag body: Cut two 23" x 20" (58.4 x 50.8cm) rectangles.

MESH

15. Cut one 6" x 23" (15.2 x 58.4cm) rectangle.

FOLD-OVER ELASTIC (FOE)

16. Cut 2" x 23" (5.1 x 58.4cm) wide sections.

ZIPPER

17. One zipper cut to 30" (76.2cm) wide with two zipper pulls installed.

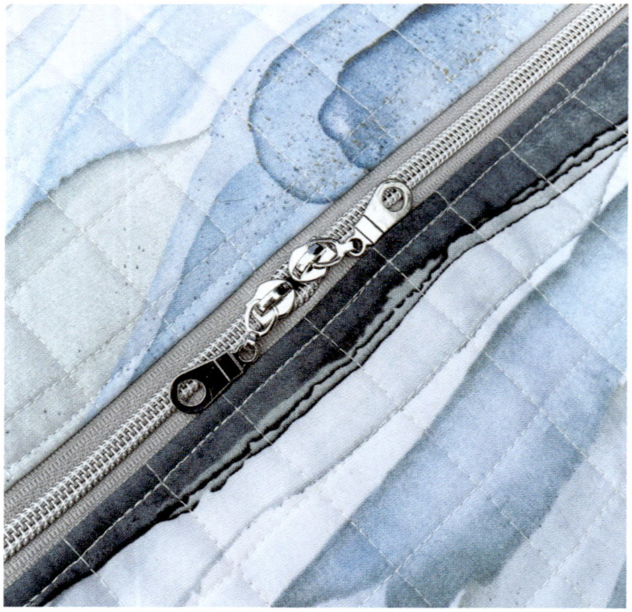

Carry-On Tote Assembly

BAG BODY OUTSIDE PREP

1. Select the quilt panel, a 28" (71.12cm) x WOF backing, and a 28" x 44" (71.2 x 111.7cm) batting rectangle. Layer, baste, and quilt as designed using a stitching design that gives uniform, all-over coverage, such as a 1" (2.5cm) grid with your walking foot or all-over free-motion meander.

2. When you are done quilting, trim the panel to 23" (58.4cm) wide x 39" (99.1cm) tall.

3. Repeat step 1 with the 24" (61cm) x WOF section end panel, pockets, and luggage strap fabric.

4. When you are done quilting, cut the following:

a. End panels: Cut two 11" (28cm) wide x 15" (38.1cm) tall rectangles.

b. Fold-over pocket: Cut two 11" (27.9cm) wide x 15" (38.1cm) tall rectangles.

c. Luggage strap: Cut one 10" x 13" (25.4 x 33cm) rectangle.

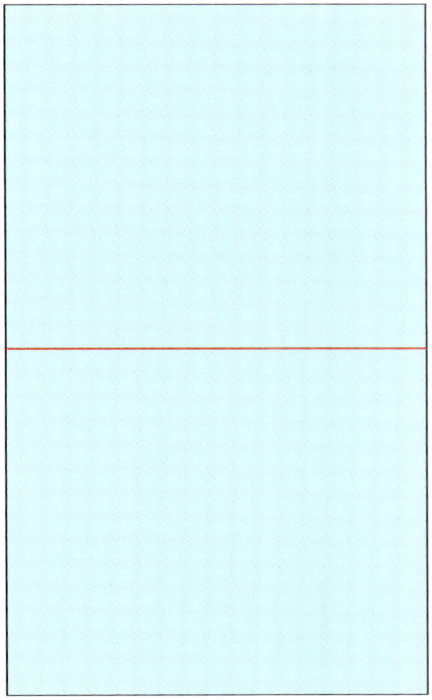

5. Find the center bottom of your bag. Mark it with a heat- or water-erasable pen. Repeat all the markings on both halves.

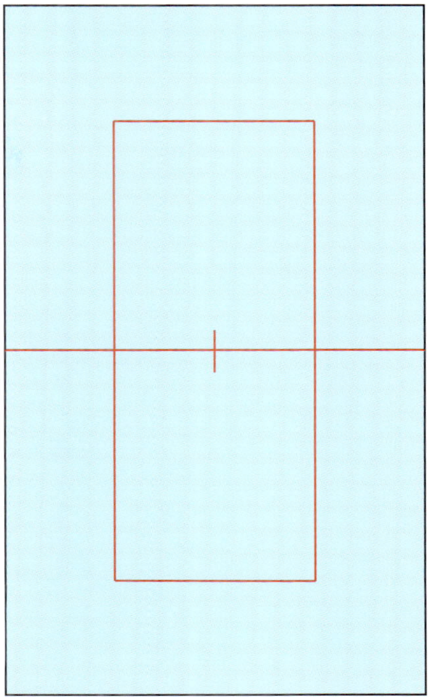

6. Now find the center width of your bag and mark it. Measuring out from the center, mark 5½" (14cm) out from the center on both sides to indicate where the handle placement should be. Also mark 13" (33cm) up from the center bottom to indicate where the handles will stop being sewn to the bag.

7. Select the luggage strap and, with the right sides together, sew along the long sides of the strap, reinforcing the stitching at the beginning and end of each seam.

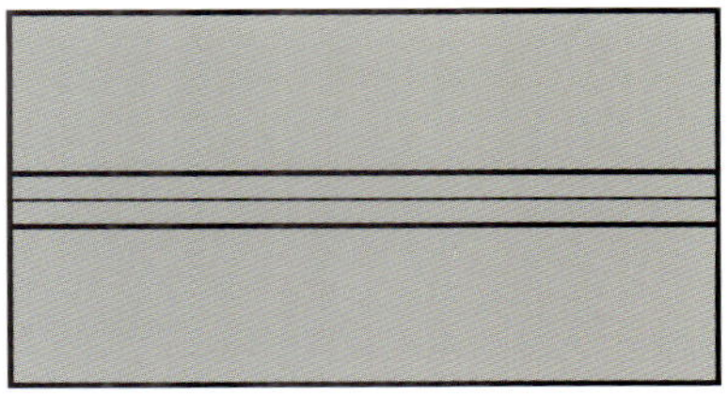

8. Press the seam open, then turn the luggage strap right side out, and press the luggage strap flat, so the seam is hidden on the back side of the strap.

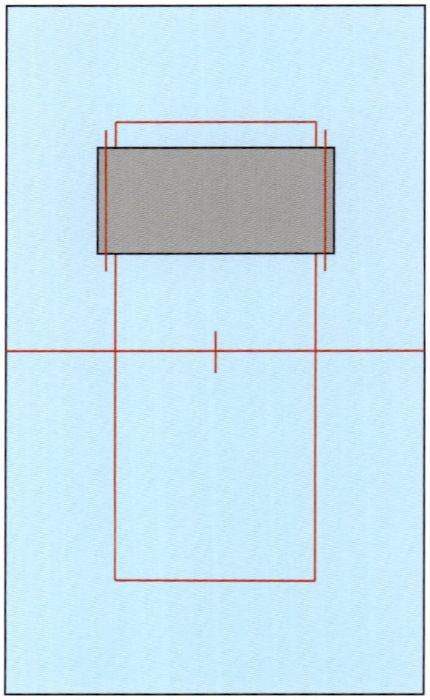

9. Pin the luggage strap to what will be the back side of the carry-on tote. The raw edges extend at least ½" (1.3cm) on either side of the marked lines for the handles. The bottom should be 7" (17.8cm) from the center bottom.

10. Baste the luggage strap in place at least ¼" (6.4mm) to the outside of the strap placement line so that the straps will cover the basting stitches when they are applied. Reinforce the stitching to create a strong and secure luggage strap.

CONTINUOUS HANDLES

11. Set the outer bag body to the side, and select the four 6" (15.2cm) x WOF strips for the handles and the two 6" x 80" (15.2 x 203.2cm) batting strips.

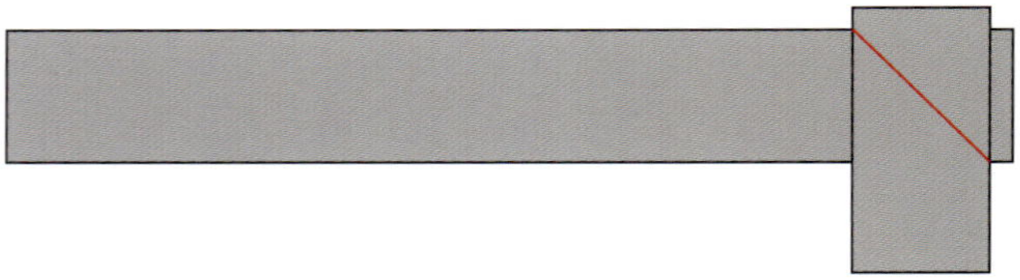

12. Sew the 6" (15.2cm) x WOF fabric strips end to end on a diagonal as you would prepare binding. Trim the excess corner to a ¼" (6.4mm) seam allowance, and press the seams open. Trim it to 6" x 111" (15.2 x 281.94cm).

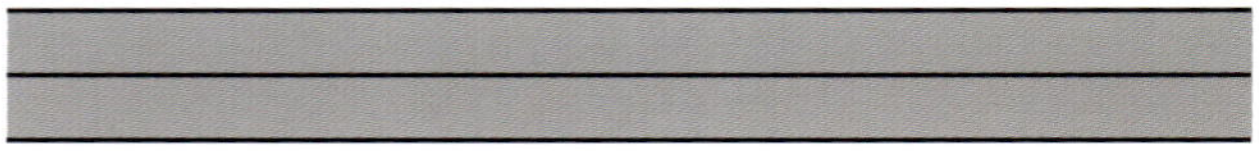

13. Layer the batting inside the fabric and press the raw edges into the center, keeping the fabric and batting in place with clips.

14. Trim excess batting away to match the length of the fabric.

15. Join the ends on the diagonal sewing through the batting, making sure there are no twists in the handle. Press the seam open and refold in the raw edges to the center, securing it in place with clips.

16. Sew close to the edge of the handle on both sides, starting with the double-fold side. You may also choose to quilt a stitch down the center of the handle as well to add a decorative element.

17. Fold the handle into quarters and clip at each corner. This will help you line the handle up on the bag body.

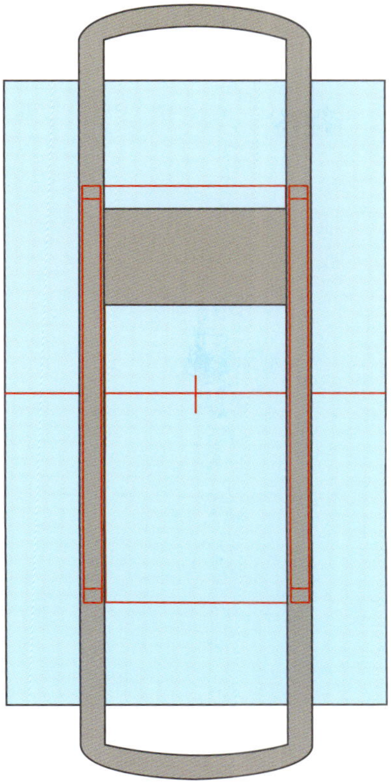

18. Select the bag body and pin the handles in place, so two quarters are even with the bag bottom center. Follow the marked placement link and pin the handle in place, making sure to clearly mark where you will be done attaching the handle to the bag.

19. Following the stitching line, sew the handle to the bag outer. Reinforce the stitches at the top of the handles by sewing a 1" (2.5cm) tall rectangle three times. Also reinforce the stitches around the luggage strap. The bag outer is now complete. Set it aside for now.

LINING PREP

20. Select the following lining and interfacing pieces:

a. Bag body lining: One 23" x 39" (58.4 x 99.1cm) rectangle.

b. End panel lining: Two 11" (28cm) wide x 10" (25.4cm) tall rectangles.

c. Bag body Pellon SF101: Two 23" x 20" (58.4 x 50.8cm) rectangles.

d. End panel Pellon SF101: Two 11" (28cm) wide x 10" (25.4cm) tall rectangles.

21. Fuse the Pellon SF101 to the wrong side of the corresponding fabric piece. The SF101 will overlap slightly at the center of the bag body lining.

22. Set the end panels to the side with the other pocket pieces.

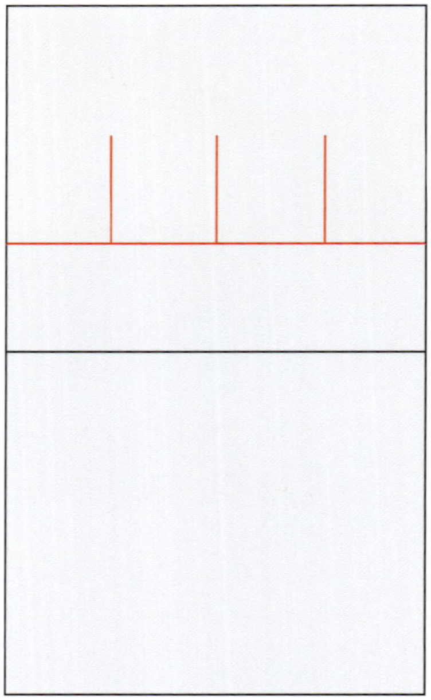

23. Find the bottom center of the bag body lining. Measure up 6" (15.2cm) from the bag bottom center, and mark a placement line for the mesh pocket. Also mark pocket stitching lines in the vertical center of the bag, and 6" (15.2cm) out from the center on both sides.

24. Select the fold-over elastic (FOE) and mesh. Using a stretch stitch, attach the FOE to the long sides of the mesh.

25. Place the mesh with FOE attached on the placement line, and sew in place using a straight stitch. Also stitch the pocket stitching lines, reinforcing your stitches at the beginning and end of the pocket dividing seams. The bag lining is now prepped.

INSTALLING THE ZIPPER

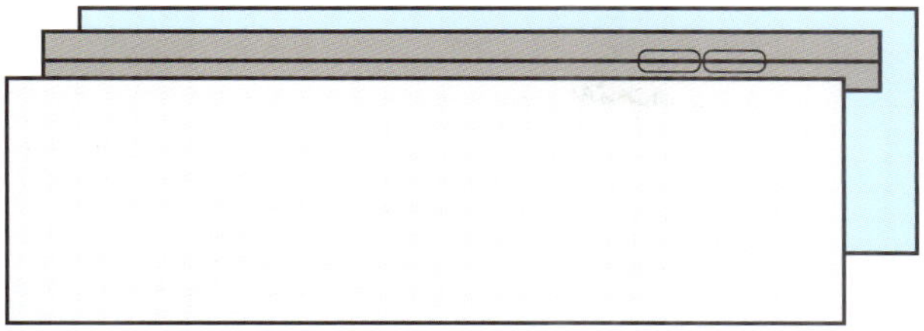

26. Select the zipper, bag outer, and bag lining. Place the bag outer right side up and the zipper teeth side down. Clip the edges in place. Next, add the bag lining right side down and clip it in place, making sure all the edges are lined up.

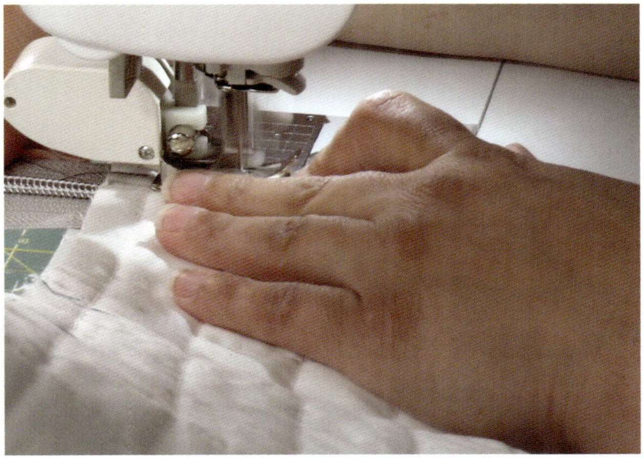

27. Using a walking foot or a zipper foot, sew a ½" (1.3cm) seam, or as close to the zipper teeth as you are able. Reinforce the stitches at the beginning and end of the seam.

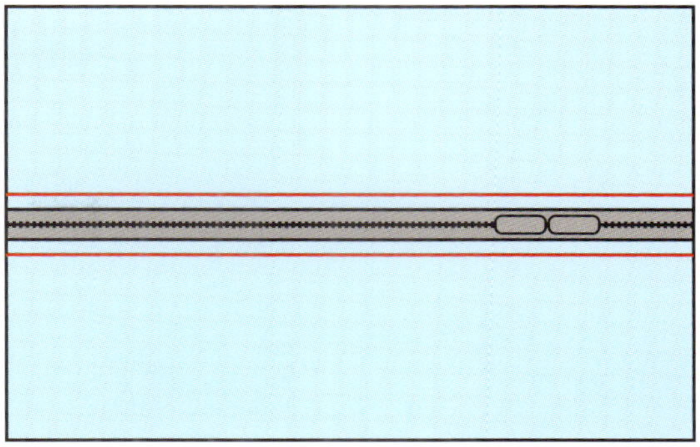

28. Press the bag outer and lining away from the zipper, and topstitch ¼" (6.4mm) from the edge of the fabric fold.

29. Repeat steps 26–28 with the other side of the zipper.

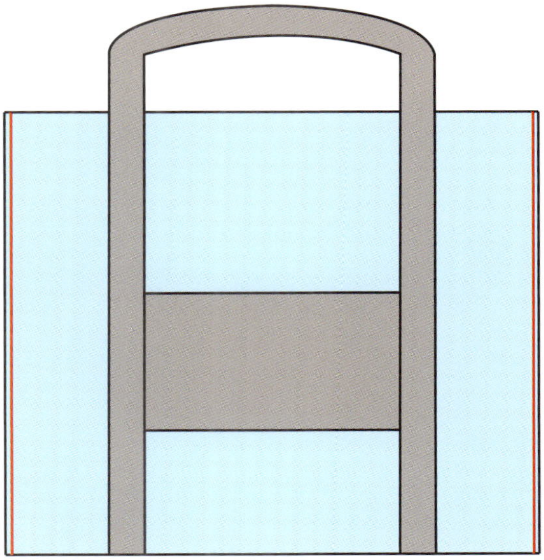

30. Baste the edges of the bag lining together.

31. Trim the zipper even with the edges of the bag body.

END PANELS AND POCKETS

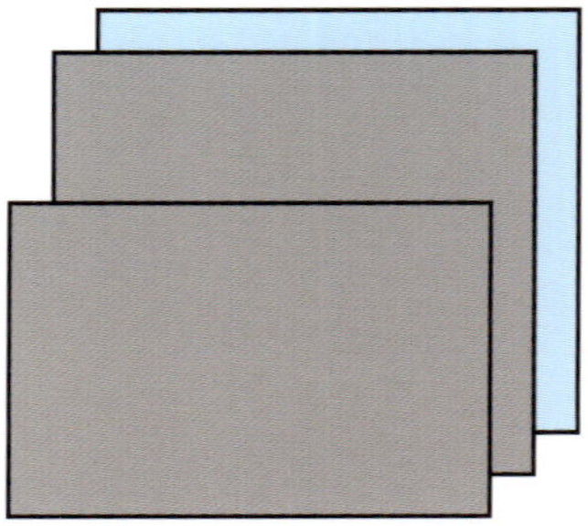

32. Select one 11" (28cm) wide x 10" (25.4cm) tall rectangle end panel, one 11" (28cm) wide x 15" (38.1cm) tall rectangle fold-over pocket, and one 11" (28cm) wide x 10" (25.4cm) tall lining rectangle. Fold the 11" (28cm) wide x 15" (38.1cm) tall rectangle piece in half with the right side facing out. It should measure 11" (28cm) wide x 7½" (19cm) tall. With the right side of the end panel facing up, lay the fold over pocket on top, and clip in place to hold the fold.

33. Now, add the lining layer right side down underneath, end panel right side up, matching all edges, and finally the fold-over pocket, matching the bottom edges. The right sides of the lining and the fold-over pocket should be facing out. Clip all in place.

34. Baste a ¼" (6.4mm) seam around the edges to secure all the layers in place.

35. Repeat steps 32–34 with the second end panel.

PUTTING IT ALL TOGETHER

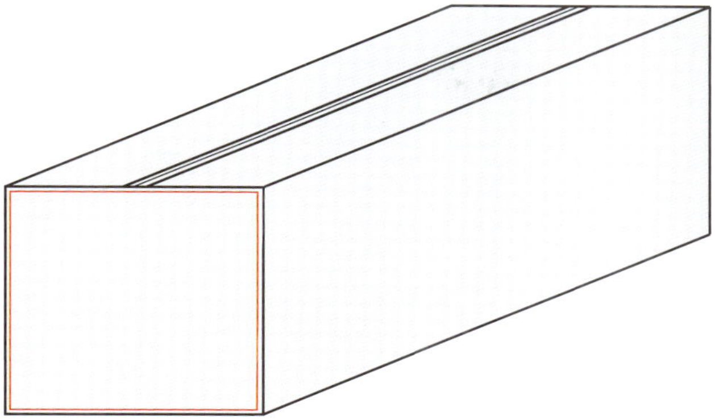

36. With the lining side facing out, mark the vertical center on your end panels and the bottom center of your bag body. The top center is your zipper.

37. Line up the end panel bottom center with the bag bottom and the end panel top center with the zipper. Make sure the end panels are facing the correct direction. Working out from the centers, clip the rest of the end panel in place with the bag body.

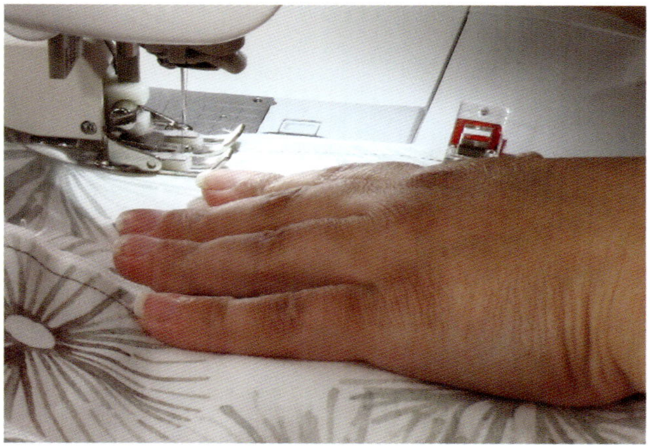

38. Sew around the edges with a ½" (1.3cm) seam allowance, reinforcing the stitches at each corner.

39. Repeat steps 36–38 with the second end panel.

40. Prepare 2½" (6.4cm) double-fold bias tape using the fat quarter. Machine or hand sew the bias tape around the raw edges where the end panel meets the bag body.

41. Turn the bag right side out and enjoy.

Watch me assemble my Carry-On Tote from start to finish in a video tutorial specially designed for visual learners!

No-Piecing-Required Placemat

A trend in fabric panels over the past several years has been to create pre-printed placemat designs that don't require any piecing to make a handmade quilted placemat. This makes for a very fast and easy project you can complete in a day.

Some of the pre-printed placemat panels are still created using traditional screen-printing techniques that measure 24" x 42" (61 x 106.7cm); these tend to be smaller in size. Others are printed using new digital printing technology that allows the printed repeat to be 36" (91.4cm) in width, which makes for larger placemats. I've used the larger option in this pattern, but also made one using the smaller size that you can see in the double-sided placemat photos, so you can get an idea of sizing and inspiration.

Watch a video tutorial on how to create No-Piecing-Required placemats.

Fabric Requirements

Number of Placemats	Panels	Decor Bond	Fusible Fleece	Backing
4	4 placemat panels—cut 4	1½ yards (137.16cm)—cut 8	¾ yard (68.58cm)—cut 4	¾ yard (68.58ccm)—cut 4
6	6 placemat panels—cut 6	2¼ yards (205.74cm)—cut 12	1¼ yards (114.3cm)—cut 6	1¼ yards (114.3cm)—cut 6

Placemat Assembly

1. Cut fabric panel to ¼" (6.4mm) beyond the placemat design; the design may not be printed square on the fabric. That's OK, just cut a ¼" (6.4mm) beyond the design, even if it isn't square.

2. Measure the design width and height. Cut two pieces of Decor Bond for each placemat to that size. For me, that measurement was 11¼" x 18¼" (28.6 x 46.35cm).

3. Lay down the Decor Bond with the fusible side up. Place the placemat panel with the right side up on top of the Decor Bond. Fuse it starting with the corners, then three sides, work from the bottom up to fuse the rest in place, and force the placemat panel into right-angled corners and straight sides.

4. Cut the backing fabric to the same size as the Decor Bond. Repeat the fusing process, but you should not need to manipulate the fabric to make it square.

5. Cut one piece of fusible fleece to ½" (1.27cm) smaller than the Decor Bond. This gives the placemat enough body to be quilted, but the smaller size will make it easier to turn the edges. For me, this measurement was 10¾" x 17¾" (27.3 x 45.1cm).

6. Lay the placemat with the right side facing down. Place the fusible fleece centered on top of it with the bumpy fusible side facing down against the Decor Bond. There should be a ¼" (6.4mm) of space gap on all edges where the seam allowance will be. Holding the fusible fleece in place, flip the placemat right side up, and fuse it in place starting from the middle out. You may want to spray the fabric with a spray starch prior to fusing for better results.

7. Place the fused placemat front and fused backing right sides together. Pin the edges to keep it from shifting.

8. Sew around the edges with a ¼" (6.4mm) stitch, leaving an opening for turning. You may want to use a walking foot for this step.

9. Clip the corners, being careful not to cut through the seam.

10. Turn the placemat right sides out, making sure to push the corners out to form a crisp right angle. Spray liberally with spray starch and press the placemat flat. Press and sew the opening closed by hand with matching thread and a whip stitch.

11. Quilt as desired. Keep in mind that because we used Decor Bond and fusible fleece instead of quilt batting, you do not have to worry about your interior fiber shifting over time. But you should stitch a minimum ¼" (6.4mm) inside the exterior of the placemat to keep the edges from shifting when you wash them, and make it easier to press them flat again once they have been laundered.

12. Decorate your table to match your new placemats, and enjoy your favorite meal!

DOUBLE-SIDED PLACEMAT OPTION

Alternatively, you can piece the back using coordinating fabrics, and use the placemat panel for the top. If you choose this option, create a pieced design that will be the same size as your panel. Keep in mind that sometimes our piecing tends to shrink a bit as we sew, depending on how accurate your seam allowance is and how flat your seams are, so you might want to give yourself some wiggle room if you know your blocks aren't always true to size.

Once you've finished piecing the top, proceed with the directions above, applying the Decor Bond only to the wrong side of the pieced top and the Decor Bond and fusible fleece to the placemat panel.

Pieced Placemats and Table Runner Set

Finished Sizes:
Placemats: 12" x 18" (30.5 x 45.7cm)
Table Runner: 12" x 67" (30.5 x 170.2cm)

The Pieced Placemats and Table Runner Set is a great way to customize your tablescape for every season. The fast assembly makes it an easy weekend project. Don't get hung up on thinking the quilting needs to be fancy; straight lines with a walking foot looks great with this design.

The pattern uses a panel that can be cut into a 10½" (26.67cm) square for the center. But, like every pattern in this book, it can be easily adapted to your preference. If your designs are smaller, or you're fussy cutting from a large-scale yardage design, you can piece together four 5½" (13.97cm) vignettes in a four-patch to create your own 10½" (26.67cm) center square. That's what I did when my fabric arrived in the mail, and I discovered my animals were rectangles and not squares. It was a little extra work, but I love how it turned out.

Fabric Requirements

Panel	Frames	Sashing	Backing	Binding
(1) 24" x 44" (61 x 111.7cm)	½ yard (45.72cm)	¾ yard (68.58cm)	1 ¾ yards (160.02cm)	1 yard (91.44cm)

Cutting Instructions

PANEL

1. Fussy cut (8) 10½" (26.7cm) squares OR (32) 5½" (14cm) squares.

FRAMES

2. Cut (10) 1½" (3.8cm) x WOF strips. Cross cut 4 strips into (16) 1½" (3.8cm) x 10½" (26.7cm) rectangles and six strips into (16) 1½" x 12½" (3.8 x 31.8cm) rectangles.

SASHING

3. Cut five 3½" (8.9cm) x WOF strips. Cross cut the strips into (13) 3½" x 12½" (8.9 x 31.8cm) rectangles.

BACKING

4. Cut four 14" (35.6cm) x WOF strips. Cross cut two strips into four 14" x 20" (35.6 x 50.8cm) rectangles for the placemat backing. Cut two strips into 14" x 40" (35.6 x 101.6cm) rectangles for the table runner backing. You'll seam these rectangles together on short sides to create the table runner backing.

BINDING

5. Cut (11) 2½" (6.4cm) x WOF strips.

Placemat and Table Runner Assembly

1. Select one 10½" (26.7cm) square fussy cut panel and two 1½" x 10½" (3.8 x 26.7cm) frame rectangles. Sew the rectangles to the top and bottom of the fussy cut panel square, pressing the seams open.

2. Select two 1½" x 12½" (3.8 x 31.8cm) frame rectangles, and arrange them on the sides of the center panel as shown above. Sew the frame rectangles to the sides of the center panel, pressing the seams open.

3. The center panel with frames should measure 12½" (31.8cm) square. Repeat steps 1 and 2 to make a total of eight.

PANEL PREPARATION TIP

When you fussy cut your panel, use painter's tape or washi tape on your ruler to mark off the measurement you are cutting to. This will allow you to easily preview what your block center will look like once you cut it, and ensure you don't cut off anything important.

4. Select four of the center panels with frames from step 3, and eight 3½" x 12½" (8.9 x 31.8cm) sashing rectangles. Arrange in sets of three as shown above.

5. Sew the right sashing to the center panel with frames, pressing the seams open.

6. Sew the left sashing to the center panel with frames, pressing the seams open to complete the placemat top. Make a total of four placemat tops. Each should measure 12½" (31.7cm) x 18½" (47cm).

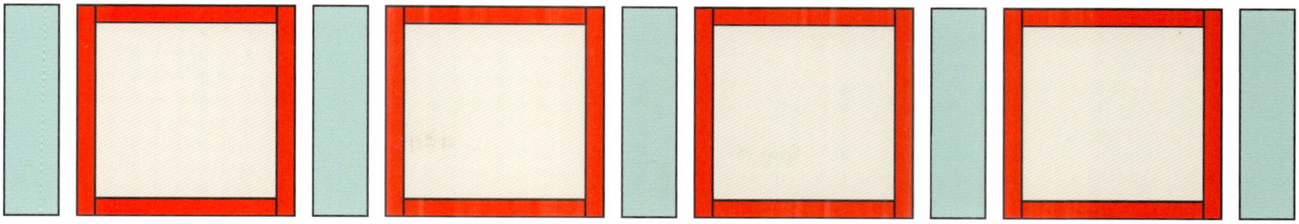

7. For the table runner, select four center panels with frames from step 3, and five 3½" x 12½" (8.9 x 31.7cm) sashing rectangles. Arrange as shown above.

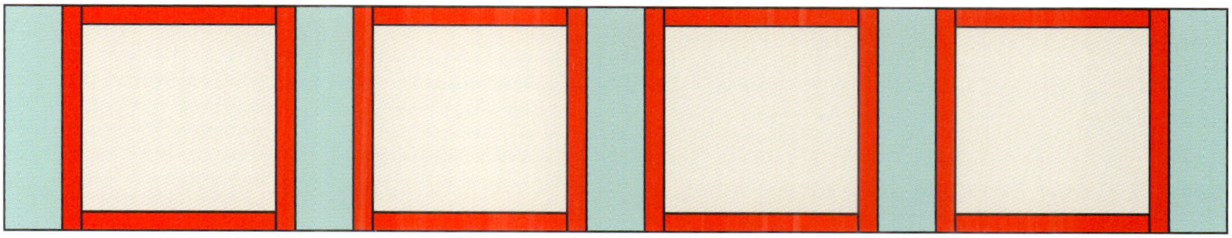

8. Sew the sashing between the center panels and on the sides as shown above, pressing the seams open.

9. Quilt the placemats as desired. Straight line quilting with a walking foot, as well as a simple stipple meander, would look fabulous for this fast project.

10. Sew all the binding strips together into one long pieced binding to conserve fabric. Sew continuous binding around each placemat and the table runner as you normally would for a quilt top. You will use the same binding roll for the entire placemat and table runner set.

Watch me assemble my Pieced Placemats!

A matching holiday panel set makes for a beautifully decorated table.

Seasonal Wall Hangings

Finished Size: 30" x 50" (76.2 x 127cm)

Another very simple panel project is to add borders to your favorite panel, quilt it and hang it on the wall as art. This can be a simple way to change out your décor for season changes and holidays with quick quilting. It also can be a way to test the boundaries of your quilting skills and show off your artistic talents along with the panel art the fabric designer created.

I chose the latter option for this series of panels, featuring one of my favorite fabric designers, Stephanie Brandenburg of Frond Design Studios for Northcott Fabrics. Her panels are exact replicas of her paintings, and you can often see the texture of the painting techniques used and the canvas in the printed fabric. I quilted each one in a way that accentuates the design of the panel to create fabric art on my dining room wall that I can change out with each season.

Fabric Requirements

Panel	First Border	Second Border	Binding	Backing
(1) 24" x 44" (61 x 111.7cm)	¼ yard (22.86cm)	⅔ yard (60.96cm)	½ yard (45.72cm)	1⅔ yard (152.4cm)

Cutting Instructions

PANEL

1. Trim to 22½" (57.15cm) wide x 42½" (107.95cm) tall.

FIRST BORDER

2. Cut four 1½" (3.8cm) x WOF strips. Crosscut two of the strips into 1½" x 42½" (3.8 x 107.95cm) strips for the side borders. Crosscut the remaining two strips into two 1½" x 24½" (3.8 x 62.23cm) strips for the top and bottom borders.

SECOND BORDER

3. Cut five 3½" (8.9cm) x WOF strips. Crosscut two of the strips into 3½" x 30½" (8.9 x 77.5cm) strips for the top and bottom border. Sew the remaining three strips together along the short sides, then cut the long strip into two 3½" x 44½" (8.9 x 113.03cm) strips for the side borders.

BINDING

4. Cut five 2½" (6.4cm) x WOF strips.

Watch a video tutorial on how to piece the Seasonal Wall Hanging.

Winter wall hanging.

Spring wall hanging.

1. Select the panel and two 1½" x 42½" (3.8 x 113.03cm) strips for the first side borders. Sew the side borders to the sides of the panel. Press the seams open.

2. Select the two 1½" x 24½" (3.8 x 62.23cm) strips for the first top and bottom borders. Sew the strips to the top and bottom of the panel. Press the seams open.

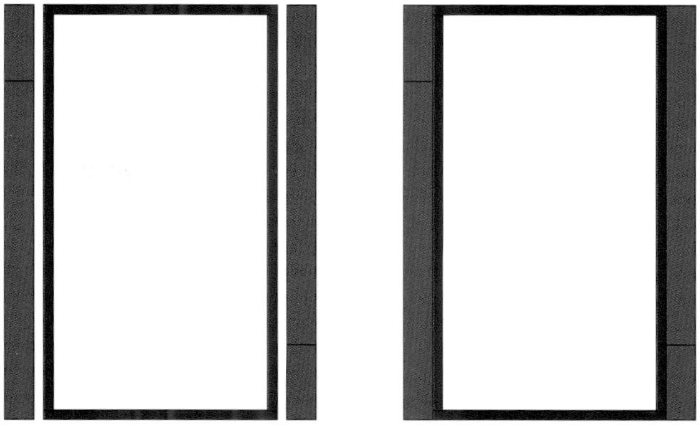

3. Select the two 3½" x 44½" (8.9 x 113.03cm) strips for the second side borders. Sew the second side borders to the sides of the panel. Press the seams open.

4. Select the 3½" x 30½" (8.9 x 77.47cm) strips for the top and bottom second borders. Sew the second borders to the top and bottom of the panel. Press the seams open.

5. Sew a ⅛" (3.2mm) staystitch around the edges of the second border to keep the wall hanging square and straight during the quilting process.

6. Quilt as desired.

7. Bind the wall hanging and add a hanging sleeve to the back, so it can be displayed on a wall.

Summer wall hanging.

Fall wall hanging.

No-Piecing-Required Quilted Panel Playmat

Finished Size: 36" x 42" (91.4 x 106.7cm)

The No-Piecing Required Quilted Playmat is a great way to make a custom gift for a baby or toddler that they can enjoy every single day as they play and explore on the floor. They also make a great backdrop for photographing the baby to track growth in the first year of their life.

Traditional fabric screen printing limited the width of panels to 24" (61cm), which is the maximum size for the screens used to print fabric. But thanks to new digital printing technology, that width has expanded, leading to panels that are a full yard (91.4cm) in width. This quilted panel is the perfect size for a baby quilt or quilted playmat without needing to attach and borders.

Fabric Requirements

Panel	Binding	Backing
(1) 36" x 44" (91.4 x 111.7cm)	½ yard (45.72 cm)	1 ½ yard (137.16cm)

Watch me quilt the No-Piecing Required Playmat with custom quilting to bring to life the ocean scene in "Under the Sea" by The World of Susybee for Clothworks Fabrics.

A bubble quilting pattern pairs perfectly with an ocean panel.

Cutting Instructions

PANEL

1. Trim to 36" (91.4cm) wide x 42" (106.7cm) tall.

BINDING

2. Cut five 2½" (6.4cm) x WOF strips.

Panel Preparation

1. When you trim the panel to size, keep in mind that the design may not be printed straight on your fabric. Do your best to create right angles when you trim it to size while maintaining the look of the panel. This will keep the edges looking straight in your final quilted playmat.

2. Layer and baste your quilted panel or load it on a longarm.

3. Quilt as desired. Straight line quilting is easy, can be done with a walking foot on your home sewing machine, and always looks sharp. But you can also use the designs of the panel as your guide and really make the scene come to life with your quilting.

4. Bind the No-Piecing-Required Quilted Playmat and gift it!

Vertical Panel Quilt

Finished Size: 60" x 60" (152.4 x 152.4cm)

This pattern is for a traditional 24" (61cm) x WOF panel with a vertical orientation. With this pattern, you'll be able to turn any vertical quilt panel into a 24½" x 48½" (62.2 x 123.2cm) center by adding simple borders. That makes it the perfect size to pair with any 12" (30.5cm) finished block.

For this quilt panel, I pulled a set of blocks from my pattern Star Sign, which features three sizes of sawtooth stars bordered on two sides with log cabin strips. While this block can be made scrappy, it looks amazing as a fabric fade with the lightest fabrics close to the star and the darkest fabrics away from the star. If you are following my block design, you'll want to choose the three lightest prints for the sawtooth star background and cut Fabrics 4–11 into log cabin strips. The darkest print, Fabric 12, will be for the stars. I have included a color-coded chart for the log cabin strips of which fabrics to use in which place on each block. You'll also find a cutting guide to make sure you have the right sizes in the right fabrics to achieve the fade.

You can also customize your block choice to fit the theme of your panel. *Block Genius* by Sue Voegtlin is a great resource to use along with this book. You can choose the block that best fits your panel design, and then follow the cutting instructions in *Block Genius* to create your own custom quilt design. The only limit is your imagination.

Fabric Requirements

Panel	Border	Swatch Fabric 1	Swatch Fabric 2	Swatch Fabric 3	Swatch Fabric 4	Swatch Fabric 5	Swatch Fabric 6
(1) 24" x 44" (61 x 111.7cm)	⅜ yard (34.29cm)	¼ yard (22.86cm)	⅜ yard (34.29cm)	⅜ yard (34.3cm)	½ yard (45.72cm)	½ yard (45.72cm)	⅝ yard (57.15cm)

Swatch Fabric 7	Swatch Fabric 8	Swatch Fabric 9	Swatch Fabric 10	Swatch Fabric 11	Swatch Fabric 12	Binding
⅝ yard (57.15cm)	⅜ yard (34.29cm)	⅜ yard (34.29cm)	⅜ yard (34.29cm) or 1 fat quarter	⅜ yard (34.29cm) or 1 fat quarter	1 yard (91.44cm)	¾ yard (68.58cm)

Watch a video tutorial on how to make the Vertical Panel Quilt!

Cutting Instructions

PANEL

1. Fussy cut the panel to 22½" x 42½" (57.2 x 113.03cm).

BORDER

2. Cut two 1½" x 42½" (3.8 x 113.03cm) strips for the top and bottom borders.

3. Cut two 3½" x 24½" (8.9 x 62.23cm) strips for the side borders.

4" (10.2CM) STAR BACKGROUND: FABRIC 1 (LIGHTEST)

4. Cut one 3¼" (8.3cm) x WOF strips. Cross cut into six 3¼" (8.3cm) squares for the big triangles in the flying geese.

5. Cut one 1½" (3.8cm) x WOF strip. Cross cut into (24) 1½" (3.8cm) corner squares.

6" (15.2CM) STAR BACKGROUND: FABRIC 2

6. Cut one 4¼" (10.8cm) x WOF strip. Cross cut into six 4¼" (10.8cm) squares for the big triangles in the flying geese.

7. Cut two 2" x 21" (5.1 x 53.3cm) strips. Cross cut each strip into (24) 2" (5.1cm) squares for the block corners.

8" (20.3CM) STAR BACKGROUND: FABRIC 3

8. Cut one 5¼" x 21" (13.3 x 53.3cm) strip. Cross cut into four 5¼" (13.3cm) squares for the big triangles in the flying geese.

9. Cut one 2½" (6.4cm) x WOF strips. Cross cut each strip into eight 5½" (14cm) squares for a total of (16) 5½" (14cm) squares for the block corners.

LOG CABIN FADE STRIP PLACEMENT CHART

Colors Light (4) to Dark (11)	A: 1½" x 4½" (3.8 x 11.4cm)	B: 1½" x 5½" (3.8 x 14cm)	C: 1½" x 6½" (3.8 x 16.5cm)	D: 1½" x 7½" (3.8 x 19cm)	E: 1½" x 8½" (3.8 x 21.6cm)	F: 1½ x 9½" (3.8 x 24.1cm)	G: 1½" x 10½" (3.8 x 26.7cm)	H: 1½" x 11½" (3.8 x 29.2cm)	I: 1½" x 12½" (3.8 x 31.8cm)
4	6	6	6	6	6	6			
5		6	6	6	6	6	6		
6			6	6	6	6	6	6	
7				6	6	6	6	6	6
8					6	6	6	6	
9						6	6	6	6
10							6	6	
11								6	6

4" (10.2cm) Star Block

6" (15.2cm) Star Block

8" (20.3cm) Star Block

LOG CABIN STRIPS

The chart above shows where to place Fabrics 4–11 when you are laying out your quilt block. The instructions below tell you how to cut economically from each fabric. Each log cabin strip size has been assigned a letter below. Please refer to the list to know how many of each size are needed for each size quilt.

- **A** (1½" x 4½") (3.8 x 11.4cm)
- **B** (1½" x 5½") (3.8 x 14cm)
- **C** (1½" x 6½") (3.8 x 16.5cm)
- **D** (1½" x 7½") (3.8 x 19cm)
- **E** (1½" x 8½") (3.8 x 21.6cm)
- **F** (1½" x 9½") (3.8 x 24.1cm)
- **G** (1½" x 10½") (3.8 x 26.7cm)
- **H** (1½" x 11½") (3.8 x 29.2cm)
- **I** (1½" x 12½") (3.8 x 31.8cm)

FABRIC 4

10. Cut one 14" (35.6cm) x WOF strips. Cross cut the strip into (18) 1½" x 14" (3.8 x 35.6cm) strips. Cross cut the 1½" x 14" (3.8 x 35.6cm) x strips into the following combinations:

- Cut six strips into **A** (1½" x 4½" [3.8 x 11.4cm]) and **F** (1½" x 9½" [3.8 x 24.1cm]).
- Cut six strips into **B** (1½" x 5½" [3.8 x 14cm]) and **E** (1½" x 8½" [3.8 x 21.6cm]).
- Cut six strips into **C** (1½" x 6½" [3.8 x 16.5cm]) and **D** (1½" x 7½" [3.8 x 19cm]).

FABRIC 5

11. Cut one 16" (40.6cm) x WOF strips. Cross cut the strip into (18) 1½" x 16" (3.8 x 40.6cm) strips. Cross cut the 1½" x 16" (3.8 x 40.6cm) strips into the following combinations:

- Cut six strips into **B** (1½" x 5½" [3.8 x 14cm]) and **G** (1½" x 10½" [3.8 x 26.7cm]).
- Cut six strips into **C** (1½" x 6½" [3.8 x 16.5cm]) and **F** (1½" x 9½" [3.8 x 24.1cm]).
- Cut six strips into **D** (1½" x 7½" [3.8 x 19cm]) and **E** (1½" x 8½" [3.8 x 21.6cm]).

FABRIC 6

12. Cut one 18" (45.7cm) x WOF strips. Cross cut the strip into (18) 1½" x 18" (3.8 x 45.7cm) strips. Cross cut the 1½" x 18" (3.8 x 45.7cm) strips into the following combinations:

- Cut six strips into **C** (1½" x 6½" [3.8 x 16.5cm]) and **H** (1½" x 11½" [3.8 x 29.2cm]).
- Cut six strips into **D** (1½" x 7½" [3.8 x 19cm]) and **G** (1½" x 10½" [3.8 x 26.7cm]).
- Cut six strips into **E** (1½" x 8½" [3.8 x 21.6cm]) and **F** (1½" x 9½" [3.8 x 24.1cm]).

FABRIC 7

13. Cut one 20" (50.8cm) x WOF strips. Cross cut the strip into (18) 1½" x 20" (3.8 x 50.8cm) strips. Cross cut the 1½" x 20" (3.8 x 50.8cm) strips into the following combinations:

- Cut six strips into **D** (1½" x 7½" [3.8 x 19cm]) and **I** (1½" x 12½" [3.8 x 31.8cm]).
- Cut six strips into E (1½" x 8½" [3.8 x 21.6cm]) and **H** (1½" x 11½" [3.8 x 29.2cm]).
- Cut six strips into **F** (1½" x 9½" [3.8 x 24.1cm]) and **G** (1½" x 10½" [3.8 x 26.7cm]).

FABRIC 8

14. Cut one 11½" (29.2cm) x WOF strips. Cross cut the strip into (24) 1½" x 11½" (3.8 x 29.2cm) strips. Cross cut the 1½" x 11½" (3.8 x 29.2cm) strips into the following combinations:

- Cut six strips into **E** (1½" x 8½" [3.8 x 21.6cm]), discarding the extra.
- Cut six strips into **F** (1½" x 9½" [3.8 x 24.1cm]), discarding the extra.
- Cut six strips into **G** (1½" x 10½" [3.8 x 26.7cm]), discarding the extra.
- Cut six strips into **H** (1½" x 11½" [3.8 x 29.2cm]).

FABRIC 9

15. Cut one 12½" (31.8cm) x WOF strips. Cross cut the strip into (24) 1½" x 12½" (3.8 x 31.8cm) strips. Cross cut the 1½" x 12½" (3.8 x 31.8cm) strips into the following combinations:

- Cut six strips into **F** (1½" x 9½" [3.8 x 24.1cm]), discarding the extra.
- Cut six strips into **G** (1½" x 10½" [3.8 x 26.7cm]), discarding the extra.
- Cut six strips into **H** (1½" x 11½" [3.8 x 29.2cm]), discarding the extra.
- Cut six strips into **I** (1½" x 12½" [3.8 x 31.8cm]).

FABRIC 10

16. Cut one 11½" (29.2cm) by WOF strips. Cross cut the strip into (12) 1½" x 11½" (3.8 x 29.2cm) strips. Cross cut the 1½" x 11½" (3.8 x 29.2cm) strips into the following combinations:

- Cut six strips into **G** (1½" x 10½" [3.8 x 26.7cm]), discarding the extra.
- Cut six strips into **H** (1½" x 11½" [3.8 x 29.2cm]), discarding the extra.

FABRIC 11

17. Cut one 12½" (31.8cm) x WOF strips. Cross cut the strip into (12) 1½" x 12½" (3.8 x 31.8cm) strips. Cross cut the 1½" x 12½" (3.8 x 31.8cm) strips into the following combinations:

- Cut six strips into **H** (1½" x 11½" [3.8 x 29.2cm]), discarding the extra.
- Cut six strips into **I** (1½" x 12½" [3.8 x 31.8cm]).

4" (10.2CM) STAR BACKGROUND: FABRIC 12 (DARKEST)

18. Cut one 2½" (6.4cm) x WOF strip. Cross cut into six 2½" (6.4cm) squares for the star center.

19. Cut one 1⅞" (4.8cm) x WOF strips. Cross cut into (24) 1⅞" (2.2cm) squares for the small triangles in the flying geese.

6" (15.2CM) STAR BACKGROUND: FABRIC 12 (DARKEST)

20. Cut one 3½" (8.9cm) x WOF strip. Cross cut into six 3½" (8.9cm) squares for the star center.

21. Cut two 2⅜" (6cm) x WOF strips. Cross cut into (24) 2⅜" (7.3cm) squares for the small triangles in the flying geese.

6" (15.2CM) STAR BACKGROUND: FABRIC 12 (DARKEST)

22. Cut one 4½" (11.4cm) x WOF strip. Cross cut into four 4½" (11.4cm) squares for the star center.

23. Cut two 2⅞" (6.032cm) x WOF strips. Cross cut into (16) 2⅞" (6.032cm) squares for the small triangles in the flying geese.

BINDING

24. Cut seven 2½" (6.4cm) x WOF strips.

Assembling the Quilt

PREPARING THE CENTER PANEL

1. Select the horizontal panel that has been trimmed to 22½" (57.15cm) wide x 42½" (108cm) tall and two 1½" x 42½" (3.8 x 108cm) strips for the side borders.

2. Sew the borders to the sides of the horizontal panel. Press the seams open.

3. Select the two 3½" x 24½" (8.9 x 65.2cm) strips for the top and bottom borders.

4. Sew the borders to the top and bottom of the vertical panel. Press the seams open. Set the panel with center borders to the side.

8" (20.3CM) STAR: MAKE FOUR

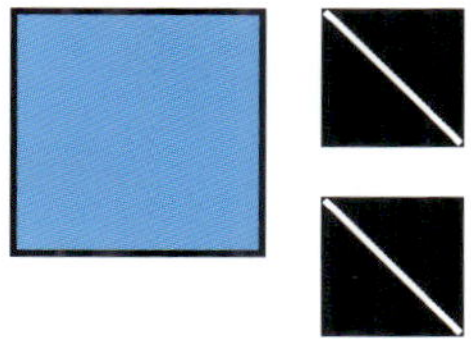

5. Select one 5¼" (13.3cm) Fabric 3 square and one 2⅞" (7.3cm) Fabric 12 square. Draw a line from corner to corner on the wrong side of the Fabric 3 squares.

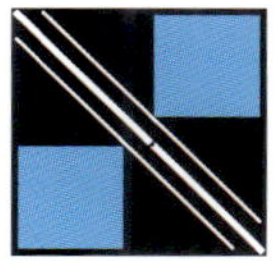

6. Arrange the Fabric 12 squares as shown with right sides together. Sew a scant ¼" (6.4mm) seam down both sides of the drawn lines.

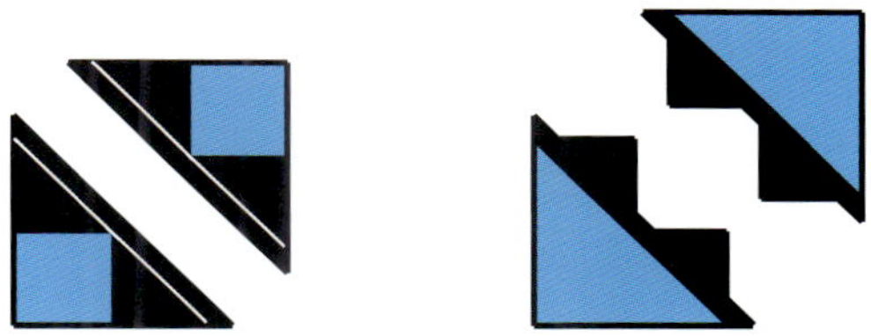

7. Cut the squares apart on the drawn line. Press seams open so that the Fabric 12 triangles are facing away from the Fabric 3 triangle.

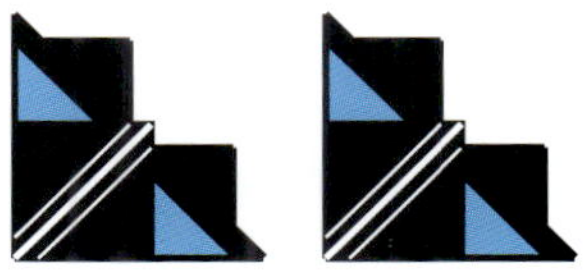

8. Select two more 2⅞" (7.3cm) Fabric 12 squares. Draw a line from corner to corner on the wrong side of the Fabric 12 squares and arrange them right sides together as shown with the Fabric 3 triangles. Sew a scant ¼" (6.4mm) seam down both sides of the drawn line.

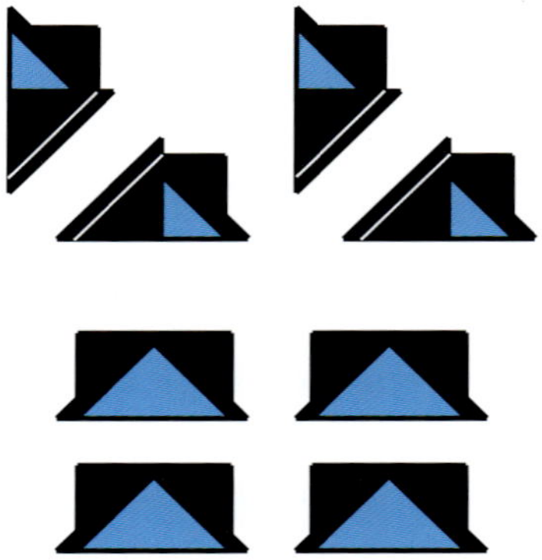

9. Cut the units apart on the drawn line. Press seams open to reveal four flying geese. Trim to 2½" x 4½" (6.4 x 11.4cm), maintaining a ¼" (6.4mm) between the tip of the triangle and the edge of the seam allowance.

10. Repeat steps 5–9 to create a total of (16) 2½" x 4½" (6.4 x 11.4cm) flying geese.

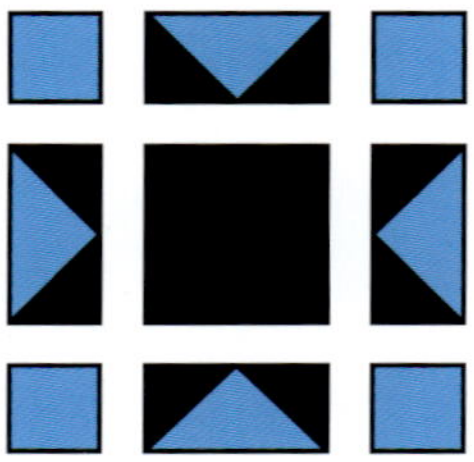

11. Select one 4½" (11.4cm) Fabric 12 square, four Fabric 3 2½" (6.4cm) squares, and four flying geese from step 6. Arrange as shown above.

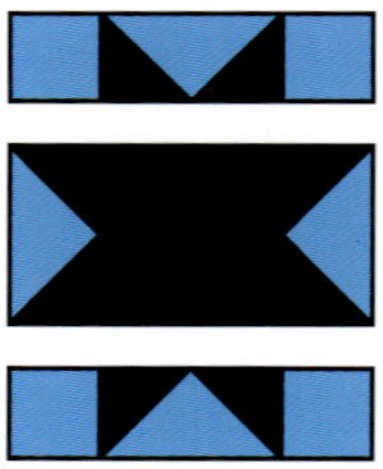

12. Sew star into horizontal rows. Press seams open.

13. Join rows to complete the star. Press seams open. The star should measure 8½" (21.6cm) square. Make a total of four stars.

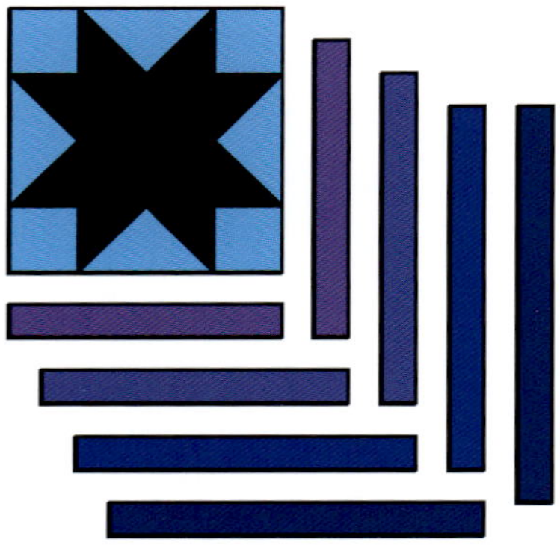

14. Using the diagrams above each step, and the Log Cabin Fade Strip Placement Chart on page 74, arrange one star from step 9 with one **E**, two **F**, two **G**, two **H**, and one **I** piece as shown above.

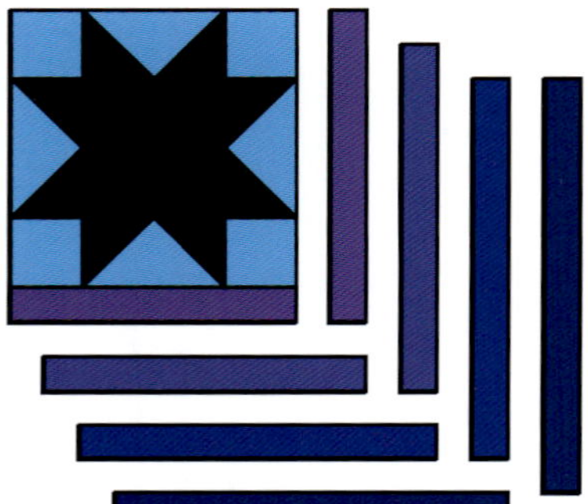

15. Sew the **E** piece to the bottom of the block. Press the seam open.

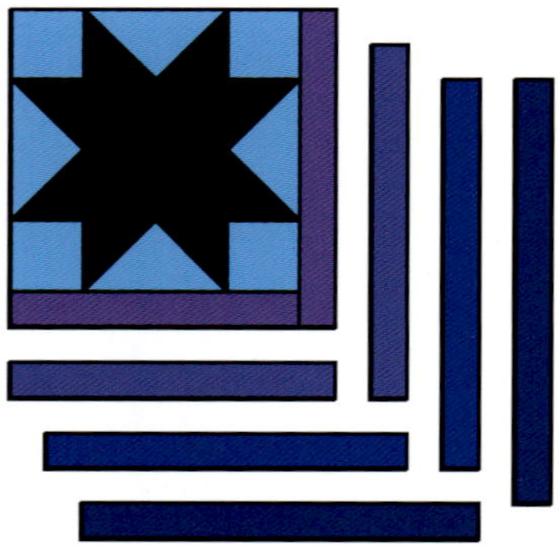

16. Sew an **F** piece to the right side of the block. Press the seam open.

17. Sew an **F** piece to the bottom of the block. Press the seam open.

18. Sew a **G** piece to the right side of the block. Press the seam open.

19. Sew a **G** piece to the bottom of the block. Press the seam open.

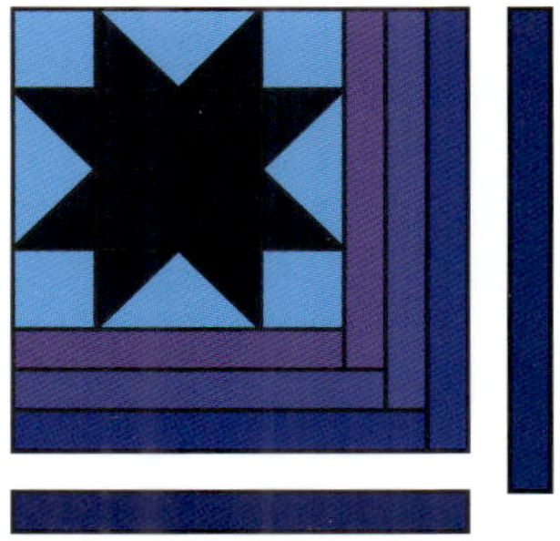

20. Sew an **H** piece to the right side of the block. Press the seam open.

21. Sew an **H** piece to the bottom of the block. Press the seam open.

22. Sew an **I** piece to the right side of the block. Press the seam open. The block should measure 12½" (31.8cm) square.

23. Repeat steps 14–22 to create a total of four blocks with 8" (20.3cm) stars in the corner.

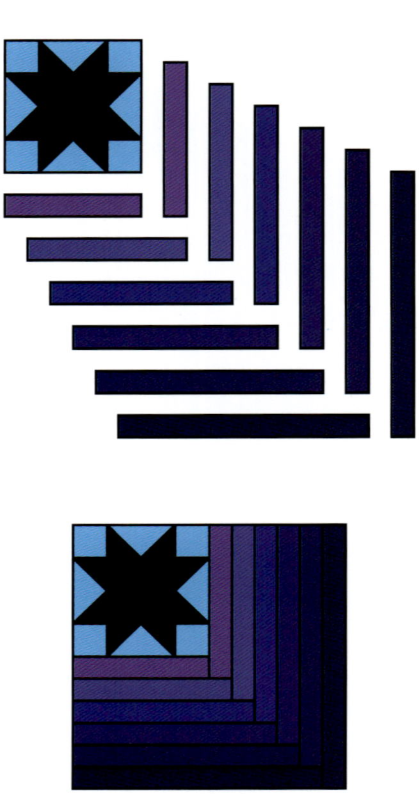

6" (15.2cm) Star: Make Six

24. Follow steps 5–22 to create six blocks with a 6" (15.2cm) star in the corner. The steps are the same, the fabric sizes are different. You will need:

- Six 4¼" (10.8cm) squares from Fabric 2 and twenty-four 2⅜" (6cm) squares from Fabric 12 to create 24 flying geese in steps 5–9. The flying geese will be trimmed to 2" x 3½" (5.1 x 8.9cm).
- Twenty-four 2" (5.1cm) squares from Fabric 2 and six 3½" (8.9cm) squares from Fabric 12 to combine with the flying geese to create six stars in steps 5–9. The stars will measure 6½" (16.5cm) square.
- For each block, you will need one 6" (15.2cm) star, one **C**, two **D**, two **E**, two **F**, two **G**, two **H**, and one **I** piece. You will start by sewing the **C** piece to the bottom of the block, followed by the **D** piece to the right side of the block. Continue alternating from the bottom to the right side in alphabetical order like in steps 14–22, ending with the **I** piece on the right side. The block will measure 12½" (31.8cm) square.

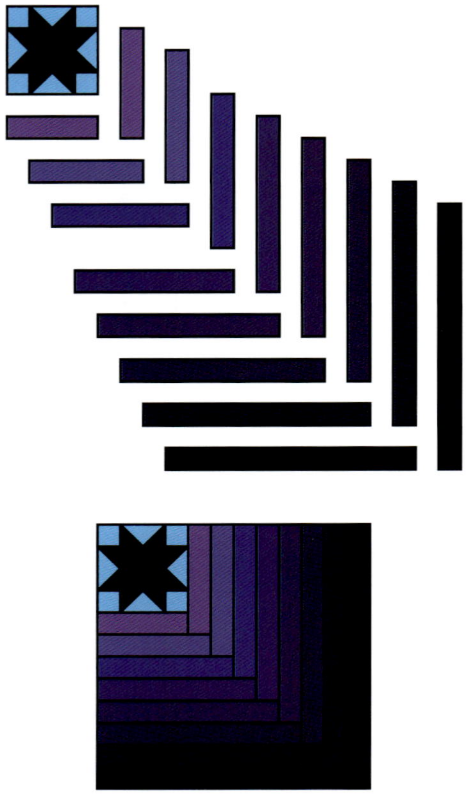

4" (10.2cm) Star: Make Six

25. Follow steps 5–22 to create six blocks with a 4" (10.2cm) star in the corner. The steps are the same, the fabric sizes are different. You will need:

- Twenty-four 1⅞" (4.8cm) squares from Fabric 12 to create 24 flying geese in steps 5–9. The flying geese will be trimmed to 1½" x 2½" (3.8 x 6.4cm).
- Twenty-four 1½" (3.8cm) from Fabric 1 and six 2½" (6.4cm) squares from Fabric 12 to combine with the flying geese to create six stars in steps 5–9. The stars will measure 4½" (11.4cm) square.
- For each block, you will need one 4½" (11.4cm) star, one **A**, two **B**, two **C**, two **D**, two **E**, two **F**, two **G**, two **H,** and one **I** piece. You will start by sewing the **A** piece to the bottom of the block, followed by the **B** piece to the right side of the block. Continue alternating from the bottom to the right side in alphabetical order like in steps 10–16, ending with the **I** piece on the right side. The block will measure 12½" (31.8cm) square.

ASSEMBLE THE QUILT

26. Select the center panel with the border attached and the finished blocks and arrange as shown in the Layout Diagram, paying close attention to the star position that rotates with each block.

27. Sew the blocks into rows and columns of four, pressing the seams open.

Assembly Diagram

Layout Diagram

28. Sew the side columns to the panel center, pressing the seams open.

29. Sew the top and bottom rows to the panel with columns attached, pressing the seams open.

30. Sew a ⅛" (3.2cm) seam allowance around the quilt top to keep the log cabin seams from pulling apart during the quilting process.

MAKE IT YOUR OWN

The Vertical Panel Quilt pattern is just a framework for you to take any panel and turn it into a custom creation. Try swapping out the star and log cabin combination quilt block with any block that finishes 12" (30.5) square. You also could try adding borders, following the measurements in the "Make It Twin-Sized" section of the Horizontal Panel Quilt pattern on page 88. That would increase the quilt from a throw to a twin-sized bed quilt.

I've also included the Multi-Size Vertical Panel Quilt Diagram below so you can see what the panel quilt would look like in a different size.

- You can make a large lap (72"x 72" [182.9 x 182.9cm]) with the panel center and twenty-eight 12" (30.5) finished blocks.
- You can make a queen size (96" x 96" [243.8 x 243.8cm]) with the panel center and fifty-six 12"(30.5) finished blocks.

The customizations you can make to this pattern are only limited by your imagination.

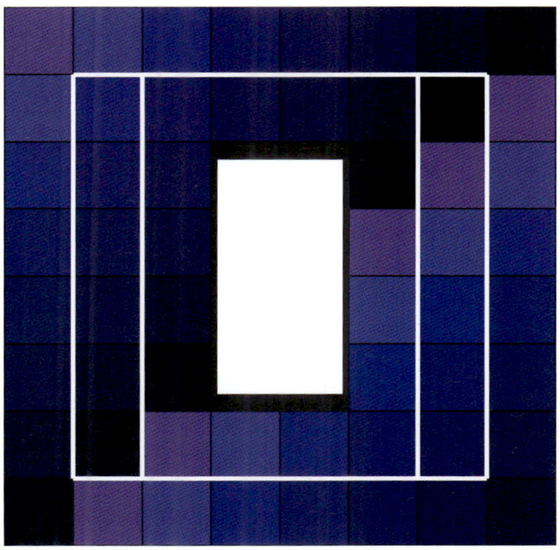

Multi-Size Vertical Panel Quilt Diagram

Square Quilt with a Standard Horizontal Panel

Finished Size: 60" x 60" (152.4 x 152.4cm)

This pattern is for a traditional 24" (61cm) WOF panel with a horizontal orientation. With this pattern, you'll be able to turn any horizontal quilt panel into a 48½" x 24½" (123.2 x 62.2cm) center by adding simple borders. That makes it the perfect size to pair with any 12" (30.5cm) finished block.

I've used a simple nine-patch block to show off the fabrics and color values of the fabric line that went with the panel, but you can customize your block choice to fit the theme of your panel. I recommend the book *Block Genius* by Sue Voegtlin again when quilting this project. Follow the cutting instructions to create your own unique design! At the end of this pattern, you'll find instructions on how to customize your quilt further by transforming it to work with a vertical panel and to enlarge it to a twin-sized quilt (60" x 84" [152.4 x x 213.4cm]).

Fabric Requirements

Panel	Border 1	Border 2	Border 3	Fat Quarters	Binding
(1) 24" x 44" (61 x 111.7cm)	⅜ yard (34.29cm)	½ yard (45.72cm)	1 yard (45.72cm)	1 light, 2 light/medium, 3 medium, 3 dark	¾ yard (68.58cm)

Cutting Instructions

PANEL

1. Fussy cut the panel to 22½" x 42½" (57.2 x 108cm).

BORDER 1

2. Cut two 1½" x 42½" (3.8 x 108cm) strips for the top and bottom borders.

3. Cut two 3½" by 24½" (8.9 x 62.23cm) strips for the side borders.

BORDER 2

4. Cut five 2½" (6.4cm) x WOF strips. Cross cut four strips into 2½" x 40½" (6.4 x 102.87cm) rectangles. Cross cut the remaining strip into two 2½" x 8½" (6.4 x 21.6cm) rectangles for the side borders and two 2½" x 12½" (6.4 x 31.8cm) rectangles for the top and bottom borders.

BORDER 3

5. Cut six 4½" (11.4cm) x WOF strips. Cross cut four strips into 4½" x 40½" (11.4 x 102.87cm) rectangles. Cross cut the two remaining strips into one 4½" x 12½" (11.4 x 31.8cm) rectangle for the side borders and one 4½" x 20½" (11.4 x 52.1cm) rectangle for the top and bottom borders.

FAT QUARTERS

6. Cut each fat quarter into two 4½" x 21" (11.4 x 53.3cm) strips, and crosscut each strip into four 4½" (11.4cm) squares for a total of eight 4½" (11.4cm) squares per fat quarter.

BINDING

7. Cut seven 2½" (6.4cm) x WOF strips.

Assembling the Blocks

1. Select the horizontal panel that has been trimmed to 22½" x 42½" (57.2 x 108cm) and two 1½" x 42½" (3.8 x 108cm) strips for the Border 1 top and bottom.

2. Sew the Border 1 borders to the top and bottom of the horizontal panel. Press the seams open.

3. Select the two 3½" x 24½" (8.9 x 62.23cm) strips for the Border 1 sides.

4. Sew the Border 1 borders to the sides of the horizontal panel. Press the seams open. Set the panel with center borders to the side.

I chose simple back-and-forth quilting lines to enhance and not compete with the card-themed panel.

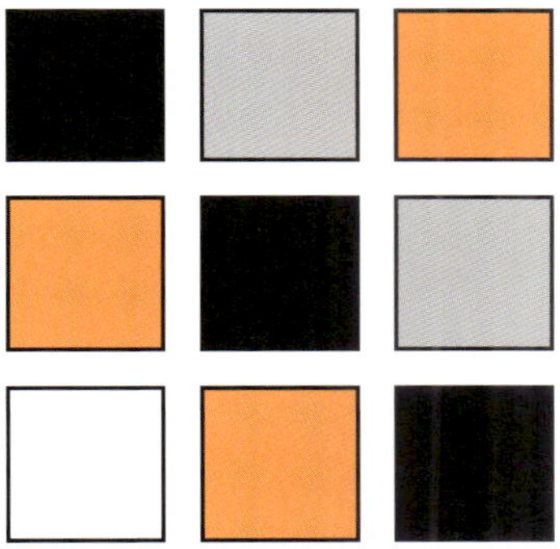

5. From the 4½" (11.4cm) fat quarter squares, select one light, two light/medium, three medium, and three dark squares. Arrange as shown above.

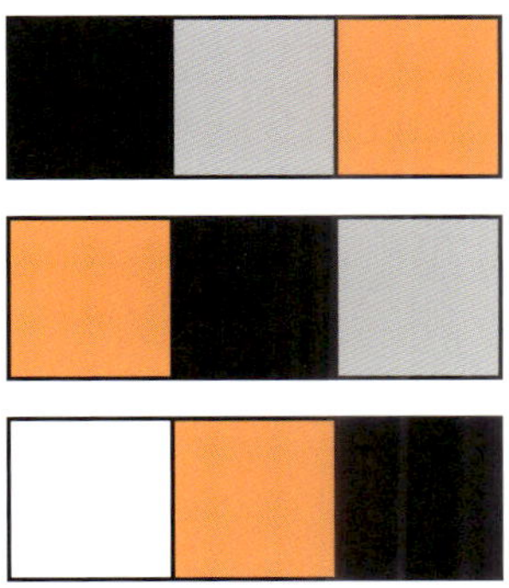

6. Join the squares into horizontal rows, pressing the seams open.

7. Join the rows to complete the quilt block, pressing the seams open.

8. Repeat steps 5–7 to create a total of 4 blocks.

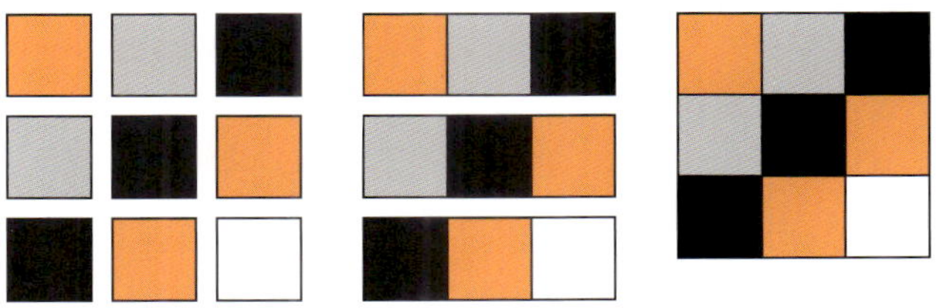

9. Select the remaining one light, two light medium, three medium, and three dark 4½" (11.4cm) fat quarter squares. Arrange as shown above. Repeat steps 5–7 with the new arrangement.

ASSEMBLY DIAGRAM

10. Refer to the assembly diagram to join the quilt blocks from steps 8 and 9 into two rows. Press the seams open.

11. Join the block rows to the top and bottom of the quilt panel with borders from step 4. Press the seams open.

12. From the Border 2 fabrics, select two 2½" x 40½" (6.4 x 102.87cm) rectangles, two 2½" x 8½" (6.4 x 21.6cm) rectangles for the side borders, and two 2½" x 12½" (6.4 x 31.8cm) rectangles for the top and bottom borders. Sew:

- One 2½" x 40½" (6.4 x 102.87cm)" rectangle to one 2½" x 8½" (6.4 x 21.6cm) rectangle along the short sides to create each Border 2 side. Make two. Join the Border 2 sides to the quilt center, pressing the seams open.
- One 2½" x 40½" (6.4 x 102.87cm) rectangle to one 2½" x 12½" (6.4 x 31.8cm) rectangle along the short sides to create each Border 2 top and bottom. Make two. Join the Border 2 top and bottoms to the quilt center, pressing the seams open.

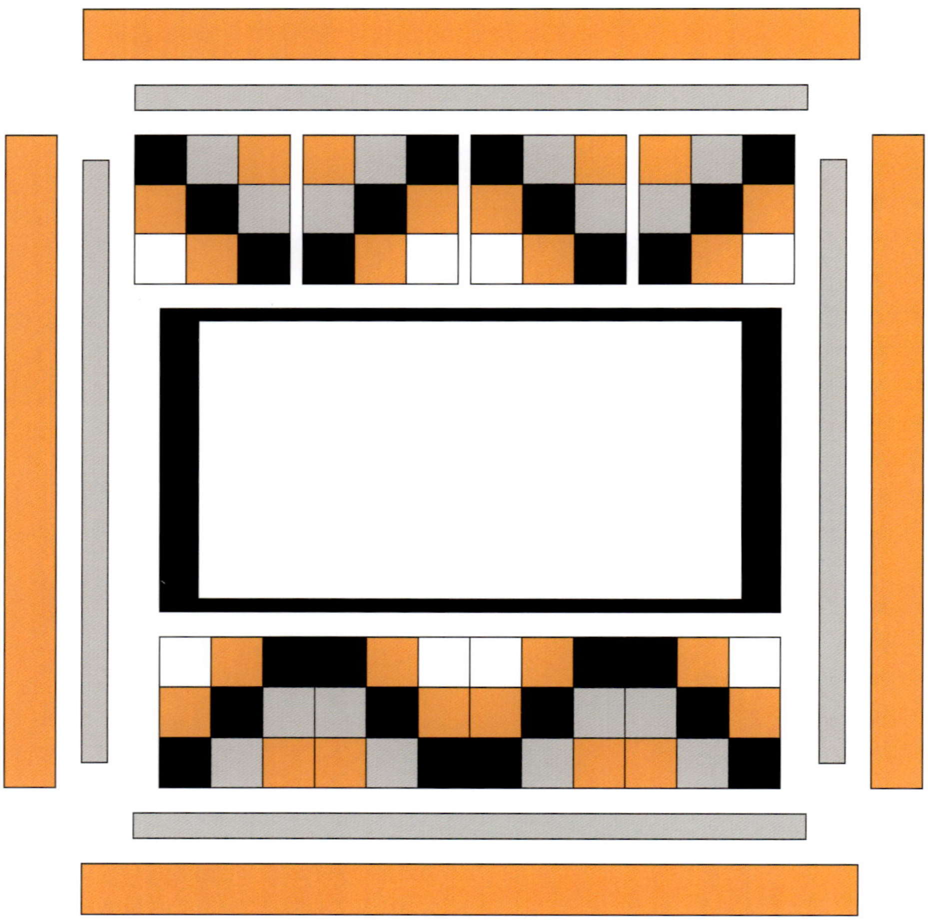

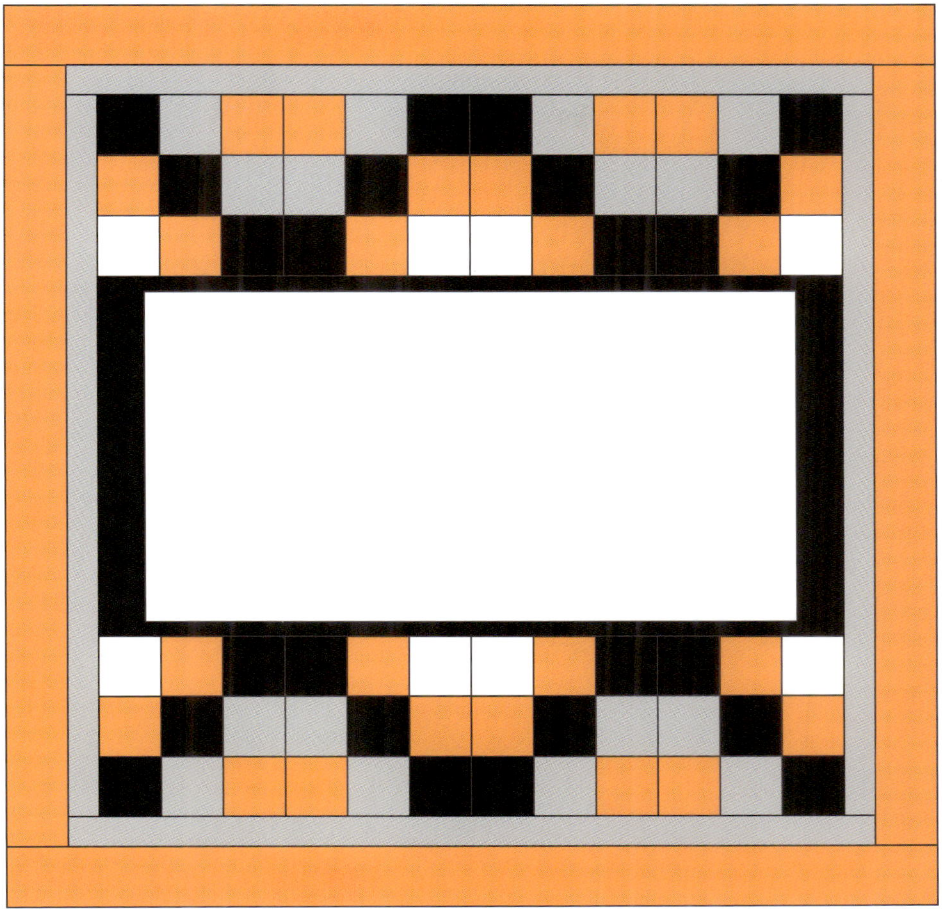

13. From the Border 3 fabrics, select 4½" x 40" (11.4 x 101.6cm) rectangles, two 4½" x 12½" (11.4 x 31.8cm) rectangles for the side borders, and two 4½" x 20½" (11.4 x 52.1cm) rectangles for the top and bottom borders. Sew:

- One 4½" x 40½" (11.4 x 102.87cm) rectangle to one 4½" x 12½" (11.4 x 31.8cm) rectangle along the short sides to create each Border 3 side. Make two. Join the Border 3 sides to the quilt center, pressing the seams open.
- One 4½" x 40½" (11.4 x 102.87cm) rectangle to one 2½" x 20½" (6.4 x 52.1cm) rectangle along the short sides to create each Border 2 top and bottom. Make two. Join the Border 3 top and bottoms to the quilt center, pressing the seams open.

Quilt Diagram

MAKE IT YOUR OWN

The Horizontal Panel Quilt pattern is just a framework for you to take any panel and turn it into a custom creation. In addition to swapping out the nine-patch quilt block with any quilt block that finishes 12" (30.5cm) square, you also have a couple other easy options to customize this pattern.

Make it Twin-Sized: 60" x 84" (152.4 x 213.36cm)
To make this pattern twin sized, you just need to make a couple of adjustments:

1. Double the number of 12" (30.5cm) finished blocks from 8 to 16. To use nine-patch blocks, that will mean purchasing 13 fat quarters:

- 2 light
- 3 light/medium
- 4 medium
- 4 dark

You'll need the following amount of 4½" (11.4cm) squares:

- 16 light
- 32 light/medium
- 48 medium
- 48 dark

2. Make these changes when cutting the side borders:
Border 2: ⅝ yard (57.15cm)
Cut seven 2½" (6.4cm) x WOF strips.

- Cross cut two strips into 2½" x 40½" (6.4 x 102.87cm) rectangles and one strip into two 2½" x 12½" (6.4 x 31.8cm) rectangles for the top and bottom borders.
- For the side borders, cut four strips of and two 2½" x 36½" (6.4 x 92.71cm) rectangles.

Border 3: 1¼ yard (114.3cm)
Cut seven 4½" (11.4cm) WOF strips.

- Cross cut two strips into 4½" x 40½" (11.4 x 102.87cm) rectangles and one strip into two 4½" x 20½" (11.4 x 52.1cm) rectangles for the top and bottom borders.
- For the side borders, cut four 4½" x 38½" (11.4 x 97.8cm) strips.

Binding: ¾ yard (68.58cm)
Cut eight 2½" (6.4cm) x WOF strips.

Watch me assemble the Horizontal Panel Quilt, including how to manipulate the pattern.

USE THE PATTERN WITH A VERTICAL PANEL

If sewing together eight blocks and slapping some borders around a panel to get a fast lap-sized quilt sounds fabulous to you, but you've got a vertical panel, just turn everything 90 degrees and you're ready to adapt this pattern. All of the border and block measurements will be the same, just the sides and top/bottom measurements will be swapped.

Digital Panel Quilt

Finished Size: 60" x 60" (152.4 x 152.4cm)

This pattern is for a digitally printed 36" (91.4cm) x WOF panel. With this pattern, you'll be able to turn any 36" (91.4cm) quilt panel into a 36½" x 48½" (92.7 x 123.19cm) center by adding simple borders. That makes it the perfect size to pair with 6" (15.2cm) or 12" (30.5cm) finished block.

I chose 6" (15.2cm) blocks to surround my panel with borders, so the final design could be square, which is my preferred shape for a lap quilt. But this pattern is very easy to customize and make larger to fit your needs. At the end of this pattern, you'll find instructions on how to customize your quilt further by transforming it to work with a horizontal 36" (91.4cm) panel and to enlarge it to a twin-sized quilt (60" x 96" [152.4 x 243.8cm]) and queen-sized quilt (84" x 96" [213.4 x 243.8cm]).

I've used a simple nine-patch block, alternating with a snowball block to show off the fabrics and color values of the fabric line that went with the panel, but you can customize your block choice to fit the theme of your panel. *Block Genius* by Sue Voegtlin is a great resource to use along with this book.

Fabric Requirements

Panel	Border 1	Border 2	Fat Quarters	Fat Eighths	Binding
(1) 36" x 44" (91.4 x 111.7cm)	¼ yard (22.86cm)	¼ yard (22.86cm)	5 dark, 4 medium, 5 light/medium	5 light	¾ yard (68.58cm)

Cutting Instructions

PANEL

1. Fussy cut the panel to 34½" (87.6cm) wide x 40½" (102.9cm) tall.

BORDER 1

2. Cut two 3½" (8.9cm) x WOF strips. Cross cut the strips into two 3½" x 34½" (8.9 x 87.63cm) strips for the top and bottom border.

BORDER 2

3. Cut five 1½" (3.8cm) x WOF strips.

4. Cross cut two strips into two 1½" x 34½" (3.8 x 87.63cm) strips for the top and bottom borders.

5. Cross cut two strips into two 1½" x 40½" (3.8 x 102.87cm) strips for the side borders. Cross cut one strip into two 1½" x 8½" (3.8 x 21.6cm) strips, also for the side borders.

SNOWBALL BLOCKS

6. Select five dark fat quarters. From each fat quarter, cut two 6½" x 21" (16.5 x 53.3cm) strips. Cross cut each strip into three 6½" (16.5cm) squares for a total of 26.

7. Select five light fat eighths. From each fat eighth, cut three 2½" x 21" (6.4 x 53.3cm) strips. Cross cut each strip into eight 2½" (6.4cm) squares for a total of 104.

WI
NT
ER

NINE-PATCH BLOCKS

8. Select five light/medium fat quarters. From each fat quarter, cut four 2½" x 21" (6.4 x 53.3cm) strips.

9. Select four medium fat quarters. From each fat quarter, cut four 2½" x 21" (6.4 x 53.3cm) strips.

BINDING

10. Cut seven 2½" (6.4cm) x WOF strips.

Assembling the Quilt

PANEL AND BORDER ASSEMBLY DIAGRAM

1. Select the panel that has been trimmed to 34½" (87.63cm) wide x 40½" (102.87cm) tall and two 3½" x 34½" (8.9 x 87.63cm) strips for the top and bottom Border 1.

2. Sew the Border 1 strips to the top and bottom of the panel. Press the seams open.

3. Select the two 1½" x 34½" (3.8 x 87.6cm) Border 2 strips for the top and bottom. Sew the border two strips to the top and bottom of Border 1. Press the seams open.

4. Select the two 1½" x 40½" (3.8 x 102.87cm) strips and two 1½" x 8½" (3.8 x 21.6cm) strips for the Border 2 sides. Join the long strip to the short strip to create two 1½" x 48½" (3.8 x 123.19cm) Border 2 strips. Sew the Border 2 strips to the sides of the panel. Press the seams open.

5. The panel with Borders 1 and 2 should now measure 36½" (92.71cm) wide x 48½" (123.19cm) tall. Set it aside.

SNOWBALL BLOCKS

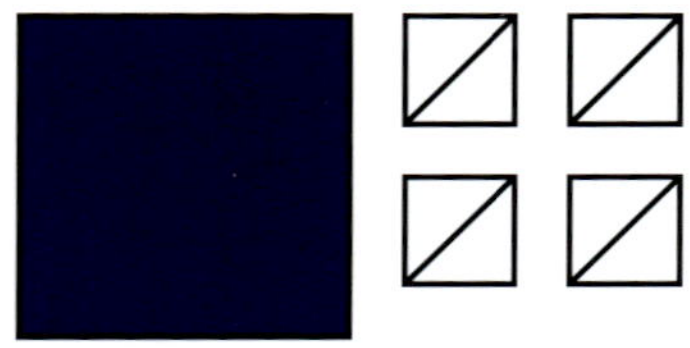

6. Select one dark 6½" (16.5cm) square and four unmatched 2½" (6.4cm) light squares. Draw a line from corner to corner on the wrong side of the light squares.

7. Arrange the light squares with right sides together in the corners of the large square. Make sure the drawn lines are oriented as shown above. Sew on the drawn lines.

8. Place the ¼" (6.4mm) mark of your ruler on the drawn line, and trim off the corners to create a ¼" (6.4mm) seam allowance. Discard the corners, or save them for a scrap project.

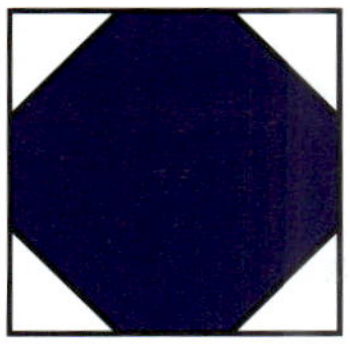

9. Press the seams open. The block should measure 6½" (16.5cm) square.

10. Repeat steps 6–9 to create a total of 26 snowball blocks. Set the blocks aside.

NINE-PATCH BLOCKS

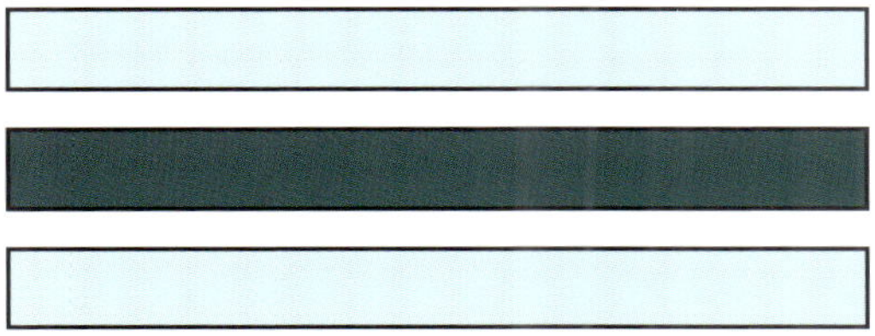

11. Select 14 light medium, and seven medium 2½" x 21" (6.4 x 53.3cm) strips. Arrange the strips in sets of three as shown above. Keep it scrappy.

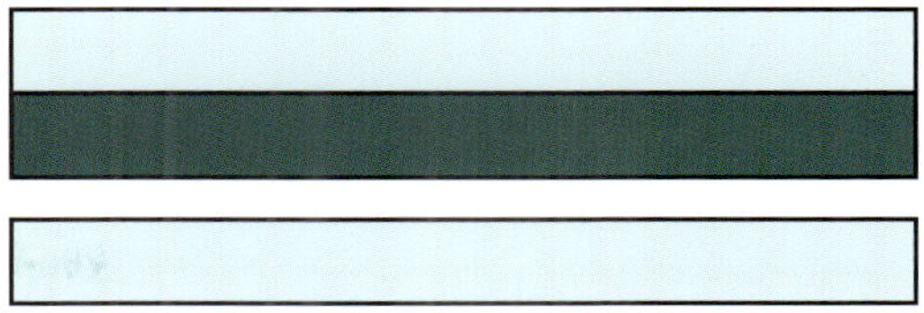

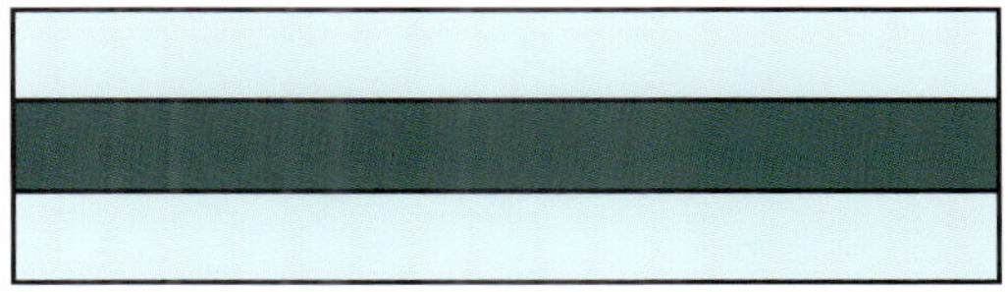

12. Sew the strips right sides together along the long sides. Press the seams open to create a strip set that measures 6½" x 21" (16.5 x 53.3cm). Make seven total strip sets.

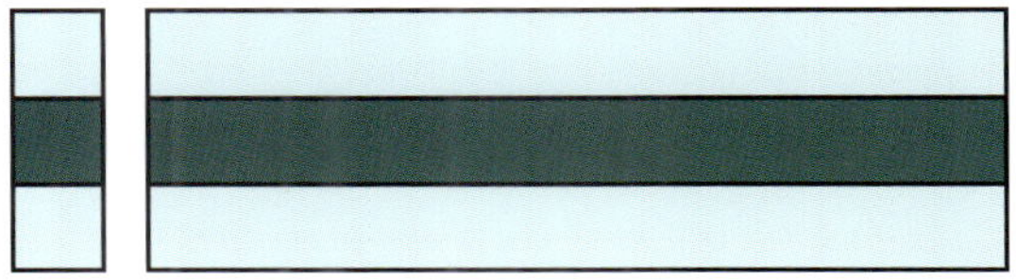

13. Cross cut the strip set to create a 2½" x 6½" (16.5 x 53.3cm) strip-pieced unit.

A gently curving serpentine pattern ending in a single pebble makes for a beautiful quilting finish.

14. Repeat to cut a total of eight strip-pieced units per strip. You will need 52 total strip-pieced units with two light/medium squares and one medium square in the center.

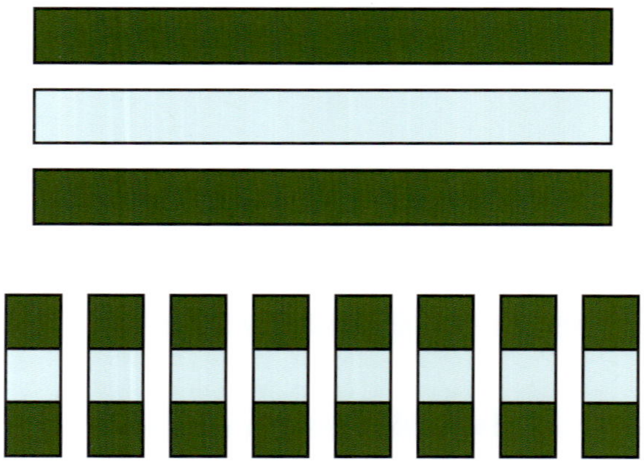

15. Repeat steps 11–14 with eight medium and four light/medium strips as shown above to create a total of four strip sets and 26 strip pieced units with two medium squares and one light/medium strip in the center.

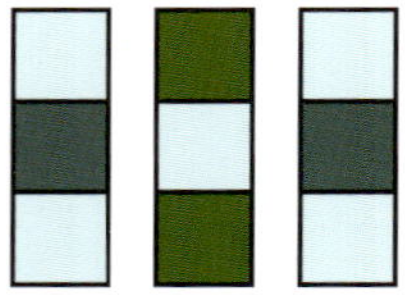

16. Select two strip-pieced units from step 14 and one strip pieced unit from step 15, and arrange them as shown above.

17. Sew the strip pieced units together to make a scrappy nine-patch, pressing the seams open. The nine patches should measure 6½" (16.5cm) square. Make a total of 26.

ASSEMBLY DIAGRAM

18. Refer to the assembly diagram to join the quilt blocks from steps 9–17 into four columns on the side of the panel and two rows across the top and bottom of the quilt. Press the seams open.

19. Join the block columns to each other and then to the center panel with borders. Press the seams open.

20. Join the top and bottom rows to the top and bottom of the quilt. Press the seams open.

21. Sew a ⅛" (3.2mm) seam around the edges of the quilt to keep the seams from coming open during the quilting process.

QUILT DIAGRAM

Make It Your Own

The Horizontal Panel Quilt pattern is just a framework for you to take any panel and turn it into a custom creation. In addition to swapping out the block designs with any quilt block that finishes 6" (15.2cm) square, you also have a couple other easy options to customize this pattern.

Make It Bigger

I chose to use blocks that finished at 6" (15.2cm) square so the final quilt would be square, but this panel and border center also works with a 12" (30.5cm) finished block. To make the following sizes, you need the center panel with borders and:

- Twin Sized 60" x 96" (152.4 x 243.84cm): (28) 12" (30.5cm) finished blocks and eight total strips of binding.
- Queen Sized 84" x 96" (213.4 x 243.8cm): (44) 12" (30.5cm) finished blocks and 10 total strips of binding.

Use the Pattern with a Horizontal Panel

If you love the look, but your 36" (91.4cm) panel is oriented horizontally instead of vertically, that's no problem. Just turn everything 90 degrees, and you're ready to adapt this pattern. All the border and block measurements will be the same, just the sides and top/bottom measurements will be swapped.

Watch me assemble the Digital Panel Quilt, including how to trim down such a wide panel.

A gently curving serpentine pattern ending in a single pebble makes for a beautiful quilting finish.

Unicorn Love Quilt

Finished Size: 56¼" x 56¼" (142.9 x 142.9cm)

This quilt was designed by Angela Soebbing, my daughter, when she was eight years old. Angela wanted to show off the big and small unicorn blocks featured in two panels of Unicorn Love by Diane Neukirch for Clothworks Fabrics. This fabric line provided two block prints: the larger was easy to fussy cut into eight 10½" (26.7cm) squares (coordinating fabrics are used for the other eight large squares), while the smaller was easy to fussy cut into (25) 3¾" (9.5cm) squares for the cornerstones.

To swap out a different panel or other fabrics, make sure your squares and cornerstones can be fussy cut to these sizes, or adapt the measurements accordingly. This is a great quilt for kids or beginners to sew, because there is very little piecing.

Fabric Requirements

Panel	Rainbow	Fat Quarters	Background	Binding	Backing
(1) 24" x 44" (61cm x 111.7cm) (1) 12" x 42" (30.5cm x 106.7cm)	⅓ yard (30.48cm)	2 yards (1.8m)	1 ½ yards (137.16cm)	½ yard (45.72cm)	3⅔ yard (3.353m)

My daughter Angela designed and helped make her Unicorn Love Quilt.

KEEP CALM
UNICORN AND FLY!
Sparkle
TO THE ONE
AND ONLY YOU

Cutting Instructions

PANELS

1. From the 24" x 42" (61 x 106.7cm) panel, fussy cut eight 10½" (26.7cm) squares.

2. From the 12" x 42" (30.5 x 106.7cm) panel, fussy cut (25) 3¾" (9.5cm) squares.

RAINBOW

3. Cut one 10½" (26.7cm) x WOF strip. Cross cut the strip into four 10½" (26.7cm) squares.

FAT QUARTERS

4. From each fat quarter, cut one 10½" x 21" (26.7 x 53.3cm) strip. Cross cut the strip into two 10½" (26.7cm) squares.

BACKGROUND

5. Cut four 10½" (26.7cm) x WOF strips. Cross cut each strip into (10) 3¾" x 10½" (9.5 x 26.7cm) rectangles for a total of 40.

BINDING

6. Cut six 2½" (6.4cm) x WOF strips for binding.

Quilt Assembly

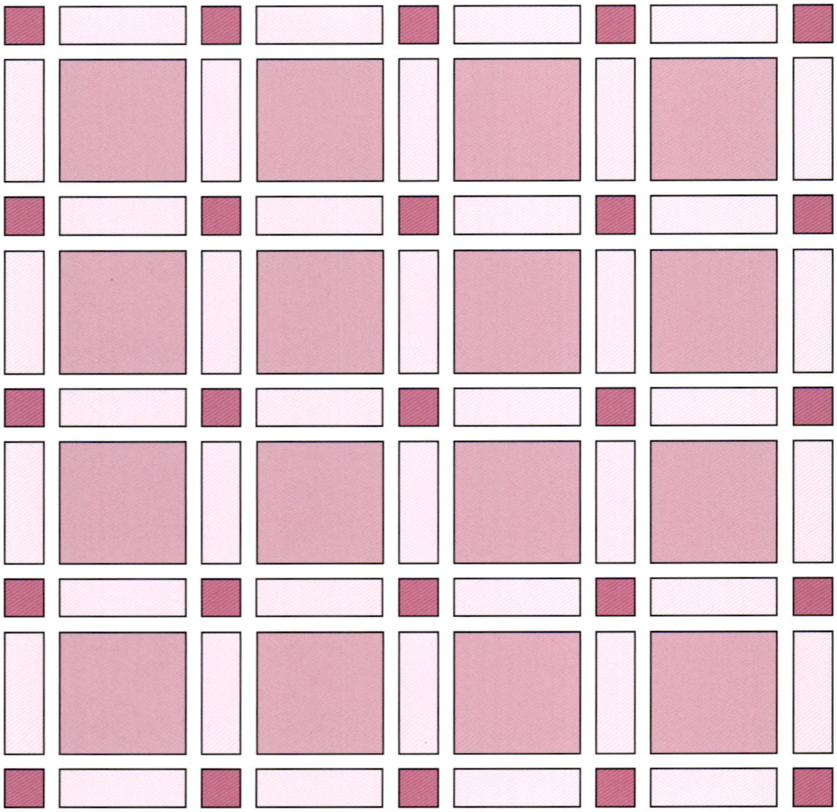

1. Arrange the 10½" (26.7cm) squares from the panel, rainbow fabric, and fat quarters on a large work surface, such as a floor, spare bed, or design wall, surrounded by the 3¾" x 10½" (9.5 x 26.7cm) background rectangles (sashing) and 3¾" (9.5cm) squares from the second panel (cornerstones) as shown above.

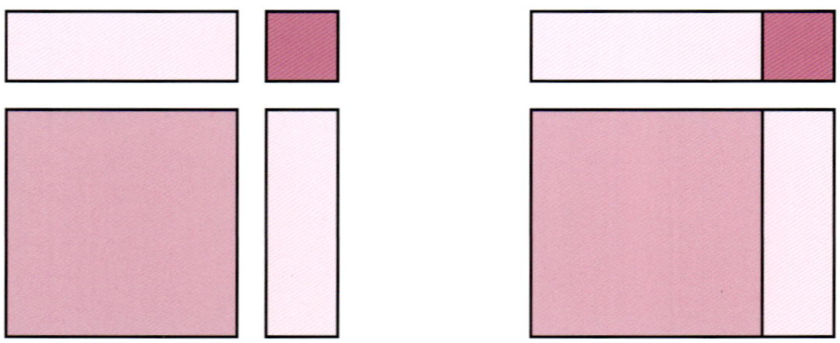

2. Sew the cornerstones to the right side of the horizontal sashing pieces, pressing the seams open. You will have 20. Also sew the sashing to the right side of all the 10½" (26.7cm) squares, pressing the seams open. You will have 16. Lay the units back out on your work surface in order.

Overall meandering loops are the perfect whimsical finish.

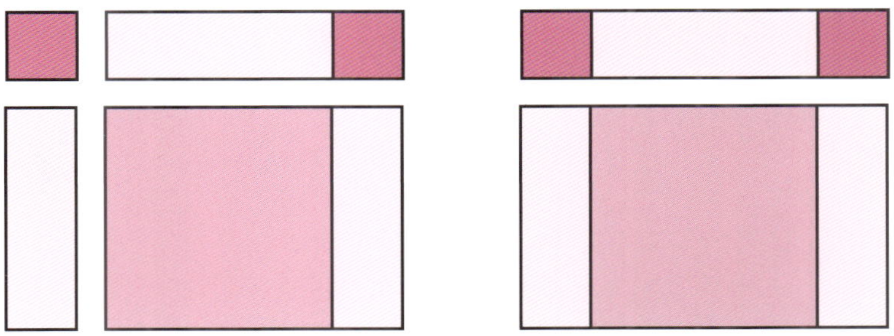

3. Select the sashing and 10½" (26.7cm) squares from step 2 that are in the second column. Select the cornerstones and sashing in the first column, and sew them to the left sides of the block and sashing strips, pressing the seams open.

Quilt Layout Diagram

4. Your quilt should now look like the first and second rows in the Quilt Layout Diagram (see above) to the bottom left. Next, sew the sashing and blocks together into sets, as demonstrated in the third and fourth rows of the Quilt Layout Diagram. Lastly, join the sets into a complete row of blocks and sashing and a complete row of sashing and cornerstones, as demonstrated in the bottom half of the Quilt Layout Diagram. Press all seams open.

Watch Angela and I fussy cut the unicorn panel, sew together the quilt top, and quilt it with a whimsical all-over double loop meander.

5. Join the sashing and cornerstone rows to the block and sashing rows, pressing all seams open.

6. Sew a ⅛" (3.2mm) staystitch around the edges of the quilt to keep the edges from stretching during quilting.

Alternating Stars Owl Quilt

Finished Size: 56" x 56" (142.2 x 142.2cm)

I love owls and bright colors, so when I saw this panel from Majestic Owls by Kim Green for P&B Textiles, I knew I absolutely had to have it for a quilt. Kim Green is known for creating beautiful, bright square panel prints and a few coordinating prints to go with it from her painted art.

Not only am I obsessed with owls, I love a good rainbow. I really wanted to create something special with this quilt, so just adding some borders to the panel and calling it a day was out of the question. I wanted to fussy cut the owls and make them the star of the show. That's how Alternating Stars came to be.

The result is a design that allows you to transform a plain panel with square designs that can be fussy cut into 7½" (19cm) squares into something truly fun. Use coordinating fabrics to create the star points and bring out the colors used in the panel. The original panel I worked with came with 16 squares, but most panels that have square images only have eight squares per panel. Make sure to purchase two panels if the one you've chosen for this project only has eight. Another option would be to purchase an extra ¼ yard (22.9cm) from two large scale coordinating prints. Then, you can use those as your star center for eight of the blocks.

Fabric Requirements

	Panel	Stars	Background	Binding	Backing
Lap	(2) 24" x 44" (61 x 111.7cm)	¼ yard (22.86cm) cuts of four fabrics	2 ½ yards (228.6cm)	½ yard (45.72cm)	4 yards (365.76cm)

Cutting Instructions

PANEL

1. Fussy cut panel into (16) 7½" (19cm) squares.

STARS

2. From each of the four fabrics, cut one 4½" (11.4cm) x WOF strip. Cross cut each strip into eight 4½" (11.4cm) squares.

BACKGROUND

3. Cut eight 7½" (19cm) x WOF strips. Cross cut four strips into 7½" x 21¾" (19.1 x 55.3cm) rectangles for the top and bottom borders. Cross cut the remaining four strips in 7½" x 28½" (19.1 x 72.4cm) rectangles for the side borders.

4. Cut four 4½" (11.4cm) x WOF strips. Cross cut each strip into eight 4½" (11.4cm) squares for a total of 32.

5. Cut two 4" (10.2cm) x WOF strips. Cross cut into (16) 4" (10.2cm) squares.

BINDING

6. Cut six 2½" (6.4cm) x WOF strips for binding.

Assembling the Blocks

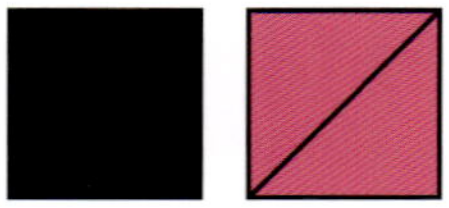

1. Select eight 4½" (11.4cm) background squares and eight 4½" (11.4cm) squares from one of the star fabric colors. Draw a line from corner to corner on the wrong side of the star fabric.

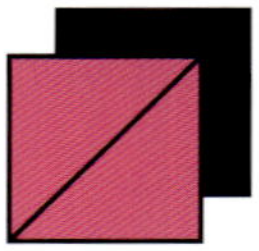

2. Arrange the squares right sides together.

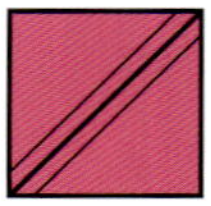

3. Sew a scant ¼" (6.4mm) seam along both sides of the drawn line.

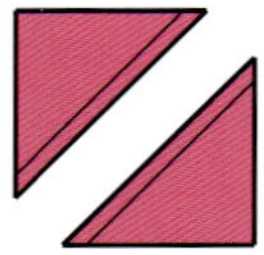

4. Cut the squares apart on the drawn line.

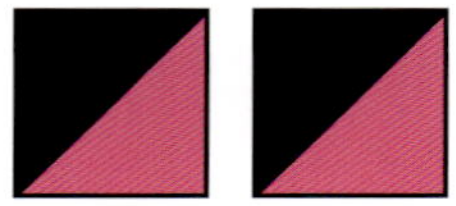

5. Press the seams open to reveal two half-square triangles. Square the HSTs up to 4" (10.2cm). You will have 16 total HSTs from one star fabric.

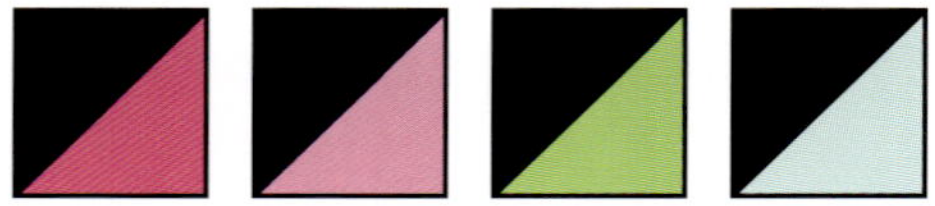

6. Repeat steps 1–5 with the other three star fabrics to create a total of 64 HSTs, 16 per star fabric.

7. Select four 7½" (19cm) panel blocks, one HST from each of the four fabrics, and one 4" (10.2cm) background square. Arrange as shown above.

8. Sew the HSTs together as shown above. Press the seams open.

9. Join the background square to the HSTs to complete the bottom row and the HSTs to the panel block to complete the top row. Press the seams open.

BLOCK A

10. Join the top and bottom rows to complete the quilt block. Press the seams open. Make four Block As. The blocks should measure 11" (28cm).

BLOCK B

11. Select four 7½" (19cm) panel blocks, one HST from each of the four fabrics, and one 4" (10.2cm) background square. Arrange as shown above. Assemble four Block Bs using the same methods as Block A.

BLOCK C

12. Select four 7½" (19cm) panel blocks, one HST from each of the four fabrics, and one 4" (10.2cm) background square. Arrange as shown above. Assemble four Block Cs using the same methods as Block A.

BLOCK D

13. Select four 7½" (19cm) panel blocks, one HST from each of the four fabrics, and one 4" (10.2cm) background square. Arrange as shown above. Assemble four Block Ds using the same methods as Block A.

Feather patterns around the border and pebbles accenting the black section of the blocks gives lovely textures to this panel quilt.

14. Arrange the A, B, C, and D Blocks as shown above. Join the blocks into horizontal rows, pressing the seams open.

15. Join the rows together to create the quilt center, pressing the seams open.

16. Select the 7½" x 21¾" (19.1 x 55.3cm) rectangles. Join the rectangles together into sets of two along the short sides to create two 7½" x 42½" (19.1 x 108cm) rectangles for the top and bottom borders. Press the seams open.

17. Sew the top and bottom borders to the top and bottom of the quilt center. Press the seams open.

18. Select the 7½" x 28½" (19.1 x 72.4cm) rectangles. Join the rectangles together into sets of two along the short sides to create two 7½" x 56½" (19.1 x 143.5cm) rectangles for the side borders. Press the seams open.

19. Sew the side borders to the top and bottom of the quilt center. Press the seams open.

20. Sew a ⅛" (3.2mm) seam around the quilt edge to stabilize the edges for quilting and to prevent stretching during the quilting process.

21. Join six 2½" (6.4cm) x WOF binding strips, and prepare to bind the quilt when the quilting is complete.

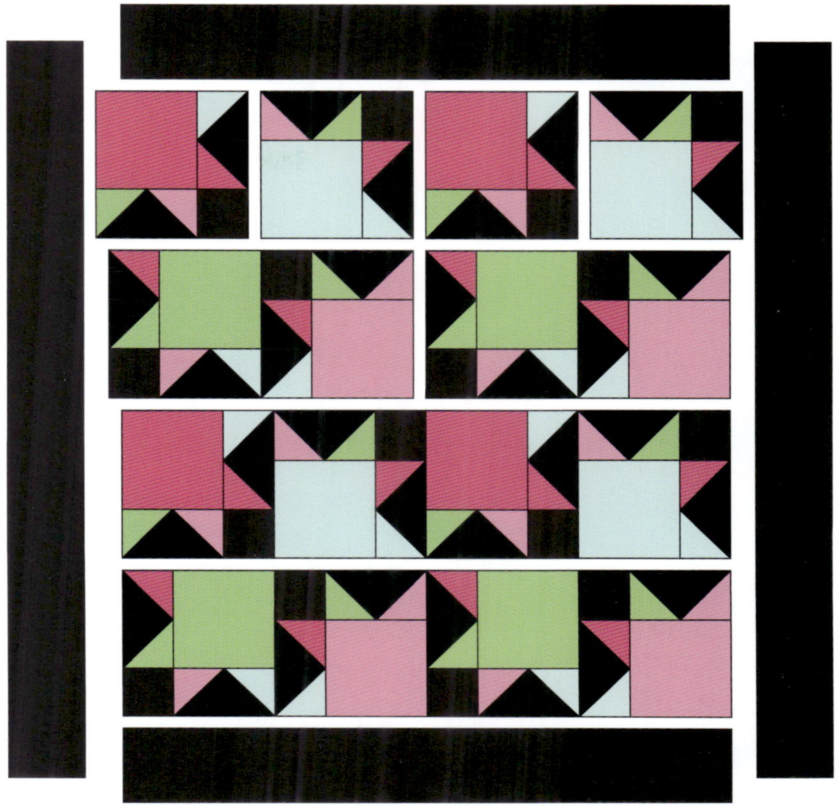

Index

About the Author

Stephanie started quilting after college simply because she was bored. She was used to working 30 hours a week at the student newspaper, interning at the local paper, TV, or radio station, maintaining a full class load and a full social calendar. Just having to work 40 hours a week wasn't enough.

At that time, really not that long ago, there weren't that many good tutorials on the internet for quilters getting started, so she took her first in-person quilting class, and from then on was addicted. Soon she was sharing her knowledge with the rest of the beginners on the internet struggling to improve their quilting skills. In one year, nearly 12,000 people had downloaded her patterns. She quickly moved from side gig to leaving her full-time job and starting her own quilt-focused business: Quilt Addicts Anonymous. She had successfully turned her original little quilting blog into a resource for quilters of all skill levels, providing daily articles featuring tutorials, original patterns, and quilting news.

She is the author of the best-selling *Fat Quarter Workshop* and *Fat Quarter Patchwork*, and contributed to *Patchwork T-shirts and Quilts*, all with Landauer.